Economics of the Indian Steel Industry

Steel is the foundational material of modern civilization and constitutes the core of industry, and yet, it is overproduced across the world. This supply glut is reducing margins and turning steel into a sunset industry. Steel consumes as much as four times the amount of raw materials as its produced volume, and the sheer bulk of the steel makes it costly to transport. Because of this, countries prefer to make their own rather than to source it across land and sea.

The Indian steel industry has grown from being the tenth largest steel producer in the world in 1991 to emerging as the second largest, after China. This book aims to reveal, through data and the use of simple economic concepts, the mistakes that abound in the discourses surrounding the steel industry. Its main objective is to dispel the many myths that are perpetuated by policy makers and the industry in order to benefit a small coterie of large firms, and discusses how through such favours the Indian steel industry is set to lose out in terms of margins, products and growth in technology. It covers the unique role of the Indian state in the development of the broad base of steel production, and observes the change in the direction in policy, which reverses the economic equality of the past and promotes collusion among oligopolies leading to overexpansion in capacities.

Economics of the Indian Steel Industry will be of interest to students of industrial economics and corporate strategy, as well as financial managers and policy makers.

Susmita Dasgupta is a policy economist and a sociologist of popular culture. She has worked with the Joint Plant Committee, Ministry of Steel for the past thirty years and is among the busiest speakers at steel conferences in India.

Economics of the Indian Steel Industry

Susmita Dasgupta

Routledge
Taylor & Francis Group

LONDON AND NEW YORK

First published 2017 by Routledge

2 Park Square, Milton Park, Abingdon, Oxfordshire OX14 4RN
52 Vanderbilt Avenue, New York, NY 10017

Routledge is an imprint of the Taylor & Francis Group, an informa business

First issued in paperback 2019

British Library Cataloguing in Publication Data
A catalogue record for this book is available from the British Library

Library of Congress Cataloging in Publication Data
Names: Dasgupta, Susmita, 1961- author.
Title: Economics of the Indian steel industry / Susmita Dasgupta.
Description: Abingdon, Oxon ; New York, NY : Routledge, 2017. | Includes index.
Identifiers: LCCN 2017003397 | ISBN 9781138739888 (hardback) | ISBN 9781315183978 (ebook)
Subjects: LCSH: Steel industry and trade—India.
Classification: LCC HD9526.I62 D37 2017 | DDC 338.4/76691420954—dc23
LC record available at https://lccn.loc.gov/2017003397

ISBN: 978-1-138-73988-8 (hbk)
ISBN: 978-0-367-88854-1 (pbk)

Typeset in Bembo
by diacriTech, Chennai

Dedicated to my father, Siba Prasad, who created my interest in industry and the political economy, and my mother, Amita, who knew that academic research rather than status or money would suit me best.

Contents

Figures

Tables

Acknowledgements

The sterling credit for writing this book goes to Ms Monica Bachchan, in her capacity as an analyst with a research group on metallic and commodities, the Oreteam. She and her colleague and now husband Prakash Duvvuri harassed me to emerge with my positions, views and theories on the Indian steel industry. It was because of what I had to present at their conferences that I seriously started to look at my own work dispassionately. Mr Anup Verma and Sahil of Oreteam always gave me a platform to express my views even when they were completely contrary to theirs. I must also thank Mr Ajay Tambe of Steelgroup profusely for drawing me out of my comfort zone of merely presenting papers into being more emotionally involved with businesses that needed to make profits. Kapil Jaswani of Steelmint almost bombarded me with conference invitations around scrap, a raw material I thought that I was done with some three decades ago and did not think needed a relook. Mr M.C. Das, editor of *Steel Digest*, would incessantly bother me for articles; much of what appears in print in the monograph was sketched out first in the series of articles that I wrote for him. Mr Subhashis Majumdar, a good friend and a kind soul, has always waited for me to prepare my thoughts, sometimes endlessly, to eventually present at his seminars, but whenever I have thought of something, Mr Mahanti, owner and editor of Indian Steel Review, and Subhashis have always been with me.

My present employer, the Joint Plant Committee, in itself a unique organization, is also a unique place to work in. It is a veritable clubhouse for meeting of entrepreneurs, technologists, managers, financiers, governments, lawyers, transporters, investors, banks, electricity companies and of course the press. I am blessed with a vantage point from which the entire steel industry unfolds before me like a Shakespearean drama. I must thank all the chairpersons of my organization, especially Shri R.K. Mittal, Shri R.K. Prasannan and Shri J.P. Singh, who made me not only work for long hours, but extend my knowledge to find new vistas in terms of planning for interventions in the rural markets for steel, promotion of steel consumption, the pollution of the ship-breaking industry, and advisories on the various industry representations. Mr Shubhendu Bhattacharya, the Chief of Planning in JPC, was no less than the Godfather of the steel industry in India; I am fortunate that he was my Godfather as well. I must profusely thank Dr Jayanta Bagchi, the ex-Steel Secretary who pushed me into elaborate studies of the WTO rules and provisions that I still specialize in. I must thank Shri R.N. Pandey, an ex-Secretary, for making me do detailed and strenuous calculations of how much iron ore, electricity, water, land, rail wagons and tracks the steel industry would need were it to produce 300 million tonnes. No single document has ever helped the steel industry so much as the one Shri Pandey grilled me to produce. Many of the findings are part of the present monograph. No words can be enough for Mr S.K. Sinha, the ex-Chief of the JPC, for believing that I was the one to look to when everyone else had different theories about the Indian steel industry.

The steel industry has been very cordial to me. Shri Deependra Kashiva, a good friend and mentor since his days as the Industrial Advisor in the Ministry of Steel and now the Secretary of the Sponge Iron Manufacturers Association, has supported me in my wildest dreams. Without him, my understanding of the raw materials and especially the metallic would not have been possible. Many of our discussions are part of this monograph now. I thank Shri Kamal Agarwal, President of the AIIFA, with who much of this monograph has been discussed for hours and who agreed to be more forthcoming after I badgered him about how the secondary sector must come forward and stake a claim in the steel space. I must especially thank Mr S.C. Suri and Mr Mehrortra of the Indian Institute for Metals, for their encouragement and offering their conference and journal space for many of my thoughts, which are now part of the monograph but which were then rather tentative. Mr Anup Bose and Mr Pritish Sen of Tata Steel and I were a team that produced the sterling work on steel use in housing in India; my perspectives on the steel industry changed dramatically after that study.

Friends from abroad like Shi Mingli and Chen from Minmetals of China and Kenji Saka from Nippon Steel have broadened my mind by discussing with me the Indian steel industry as part of their global strategies. Without knowing them I would never have been alerted to the many prospects which the Indian steel industry holds for global investments and which are overlooked totally in policy-making exercises.

My colleagues have formed a wall of support for me. Shri R.K. Bagchi, Director, NISST actually assures me that I do know some essentials of technology despite being an economist. Dr Vijay Goel gave me the precious archival material of JPC papers and Mr R.S. Jangid, Ms Renu Sharma, Mr V.M.Ganesh and Mr A. Parameswaran have filled in many gaps in my knowledge. Mr Varesh Sachdeva and Krishna Rao, who have long left the country for better pastures in the USA, were the first ones who taught me the steel industry right in the first week of my joining work. I cannot thank them enough. My special thanks will go to Dr Sunil Gupta, my office colleague, for being my partner in crime. We have done almost all the major studies of the steel industry together and undertaken many deadly adventures together inside of government offices where Dr Gupta has always had a way of extracting classified documents. Dr A.S. Firoz, my boss for much of my time in office, has never really imposed ideas or discipline and his policy of live and let live has given me the breathing space that I needed for writing the book.

This book contains perspectives which have drawn from development studies and the political economy, especially regarding natural resources, sustainability and skills and technology, and my friend Dr Madhusree Banerjee, a development specialist and a consultant with the World Bank, must be credited with much of the input. Dr Ranjita Mohanty and I always have long telephonic exchanges around profound matters regarding capitalist growth and tribal autonomy, especially in Odisha, where many of our steel plants are located. Many times we have questioned whether we need to make all that much of steel if it costs so much in terms of lost livelihoods and damaged ecology. Prof Rakesh Batabyal, historian and media professional, who was raised in the Bokaro Steel City and who has a Nehruvian perspective to steel, has been able to temper much of the excitement about global capital that I had in the earlier days of economic liberalization.

There are some regrets as well, especially in the memory of Shri Surinder Dewan, who reposed enormous faith in my capabilities. I never rose to fulfil his expectations while he lived and now that he is no more, I miss his wisdom in every moment of my engagements with the steel industry. I wish Shri R.K. Chatterjee, who championed my cause zealously in the organization in his incumbency as the Chief of Personnel and Administration and Finance, had lived to see my work in print.

Introduction

The book that follows concerns the various dilemmas that I, as a policy economist of steel, have faced and suffered in the three decades of my life in the Joint Plant Committee, hereafter the JPC. The JPC was set up in 1964 to "fix" prices of the steel items sold to Indian consumers; though, the JPC never really controlled the prices of steel, it calculated the fair prices of steel and suggested that the steel plants under the Steel Authority of India, or SAIL, the public sector holding company, and the only private sector company, Tata Iron and Steel Company, or TISCO, should follow them. These prices did what prices always do, namely decide what to produce, how much to produce, for whom to produce, how to produce and even when to produce. The JPC, despite being an entity set up by the Government of India, was mandated to play the understudy of the yet to develop market forces and not to curb the free market. To the best of my knowledge, the JPC is a unique organization that does not have a counterpart anywhere else in the world.

The prices are crucial for what is known as the allocative functions in economics, which direct resources into production. The JPC behaved like the market, where the market was absent. It was not set up to control the steel industry, but to assist in the decontrol of the steel industry; to match production to the demands of the consumers, to suggest the product mix of the steel plants in a manner such that they could optimize their profits and to fix prices (in such a manner so that the steel plants could expand their capacities, modernize existing facilities and develop new products). Indeed, the JPC was constituted by the Government of India following the recommendations of the Raj Committee, set up specifically for the purposes of decontrolling the steel industry. What emerged, then, was the present structure of the steel industry with large integrated steel plants with captive mineral resources and a slew of smaller firms that filled up the blanks between consumer demand and supply of steel. The small and the large sectors complemented each other, and even cooperated on many occasions when the large plants produced the semis and the smaller ones rolled them out, with the former the most competitive in producing semis, and the latter more competitive in merely rolling.

The economic liberalization changed aspirations and raised greed. The two segments that had remained respectfully apart from each other now invaded each other's territories, in order to move up the value chain, or to integrate backwards to maximize margins. Such invasion into each other's territories led to expansions in capacities that soon became excessive; a nicely fitting steel industry became oversized and obese. Everybody in the steel business wanted to expand capacities, forward as well as backward. Traders wanted to become steel processors; steel processors wanted to make steel; and those who melted scrap to make billets now wanted to put up larger facilities to be able to roll out wide sheets, then process them as far as possible (for use by the final consumers of steel). The investments for the steel industry came from various activities: Amrit Steel used to be a dairy, packaging milk, Ruchi Strips used to be a soy oil pressing company, Action Steel was a shoe company and so on; everybody rushed into steel because the profits from steel were relatively higher than in industries, like the food industry, or the consumer goods industry and expectedly so, because the capacity restrictions in the steel industry during the days of industrial licensing were more severe. However, the progress of liberalization capacities surged and these pushed down the prices in the market, depressed margins and eventually decelerated the growth of technology that made steel in India uncompetitive; this ultimately made the producers lose out on export markets and become vulnerable to imports that were cheaper. A steel industry that thrived on import substitution now fell to cheap imports.

The idea of overcapacity is surprising in India. The Indian steel industry, since the time before independence, has struggled to match its productive capacity with the needs of its end users; indeed, when the steel industry was liberalized, India could not produce enough steel and investors were cajoled with hopes of a future with an insatiable growth in the demand for steel. But around 2012, demand that used to reflect a healthy appetite for steel became sluggish. The policy makers were caught off guard, having measured their worth for so long by forecasting hopes of a cantering market, and they did not know how to handle the bitter truth staring at their faces, namely the need to cut excess capacity. This book suggests that for the policy makers, there is still much to do, other than to promote the great lie of runaway demand; they can plan for technology growth, improve performance, promote steel processing, plan for niche products and help expand the demand for steel. Growth need not only mean a monotonic growth of capacities; it can mean a deeper differentiation in the steel industry, a development of capacity coordination, product differentiation, technology growth, improvement in operational parameters and so many other things. Unfortunately, for India, the policy makers seem to see the addition of capacities as the only growth path. This book is an attempt to redirect the attention of the policy bodies into considering development of things other than adding tonnage, such as product differentiation, improving technology, management of energy, waste reduction and recycling of steel and many other ideas that improve upon the given quantities of steel produced, rather than expanding into stagnant markets to collect bad debts and encounter bankruptcy.

The aim of the book that follows is not a mere description of the Indian steel industry, nor its pure and simple relationship with the government in terms of subsidies and tax sops, or an absence of these. The book intends to analyze the processes by which an industry like steel, with an invested capital close to a 56 billion USD, can fall to bad loans, flattened profits, closures and technological incompetence, especially when the producers wish to grow in the steel business, and the steel industry has a dedicated Ministry, a Cabinet-ranking Minister and a full-fledged body like the JPC. Where are we going wrong?

1   Issues facing the steel industry

Steel, as the cliché goes, is the material of modern industrial civilization. We have steel everywhere, in the machines that are set up in our factories, in our railway tracks, wagons and carriages, in our automobiles and airplanes, in our high-rise buildings, in our cooking vessels, refrigerators, washing machines and dishwashers, in our paper clips and pins and needles, in the staplers and scissors; in short everything upon which the modern world runs is made of steel. Without steel, our gadgets would not be able to use electricity, and without electricity as our driving energy, we will not have our elevators and escalators, appliances like toasters, grills, washers, grinders, epilators and shavers, each of them made of steel. Steel, in other words, is as essential for our material world as food is to the organic world of living bodies. The economy of steel is as important as that of food. It is important that nations keep on producing steel just as they would keep on producing food. Like the production of food, most economies aim at self-sufficiency of steel and many countries, especially those like the United States of America, would go on producing steel even if that meant increasing protection against imports; some, like China, insist on producing more and more steel, even if its banks have gone bankrupt absorbing the losses.

Iron was discovered some 4,000 years ago, which helped human societies to manufacture a variety to tools for cutting down trees, clearing forests, ploughing fields and hunting down animals; steel is the very foundation of the industrial age not merely for the tools and machines, but to literally "contain" human bodies in their concrete homes, passenger cars, trains, boats, ships and airplanes. Iron that is used for making tools is cast, while the steel with which automobiles are made and tall buildings are raised is rolled, steel being a compound of iron and carbon. Iron is extracted from ore (by the use of oxygen in the presence of heat), while steel has to be made out of iron by adding carbon to iron in a molten state, known as hot metal. Steel has two major properties, namely malleability, which means that steel can be rolled out into sheets, and ductility, by which steel can be drawn out into wires. Most of the technological innovations in steel try to increase the two properties of the materials. Steel is a compound of iron and carbon, with other elements contained in traces. However, the basic form of steel, sometimes known as carbon steel or mild steel, is a compound of iron and carbon - carbon constituting anywhere from 0.05% to 0.25% of the weight of the compound.

One can add manganese, silicon, nickel and other metals, depending on what kind of compound one needs. Steel, when compounded with other metals, becomes ready for specialized uses, such as in machine parts, surgical instruments, auto components and so on. Industrial steel is, of course, mild steel, which contains about 0.25% carbon and little of any other metals. Only mild steel is malleable and ductile.

Reading through the book *Guns, Germs and Steel* by Jared Diamond,[1] one is struck by the observation that hominids knew and practiced metallurgy before they even knew and organized farming and agriculture. While food growing appears to be solely the preserve of the homo sapiens, metallurgy may have also existed among the other hominids, the Homo Habilis being worthy of mention among them. Jacob Bronowski's book, *Ascent of Man*, mentions that metallurgy came almost at the same time as the discovery of fire, something that many hominids knew of.[2] Jack Goody's book, *Metals, Culture and Capitalism*, mentions that metallurgy predated cultivation, rather than the other way a round, though the order of metals may not always have been mercury, copper, bronze and iron. Indeed, Goody mentions that Africa knew iron making before it had handled any other kind of metal, and seems to have completely bypassed the copper stage. The sum and substance of this is to say that metallurgy is an ancient practice of mankind and that steel by no means appears to be a new metal discovered suddenly by human civilization in its industrial age.[3]

The Industrial Revolution made the production of large quantities of steel possible and also, the production of the malleable and ductile kind of materials that then increased the possibilities of new uses. The development of the railways and the locomotive industry used up these large volumes of steel. Soon, everything was large scale, organized in factories and assembly lines and steel was used for building machines, cities and taller buildings, especially those which used concrete reinforcements. In the 20th century, both war and reconstruction of sites devastated by the war became large users of steel. The discovery of oil as the major source of energy brought in the use of large diameter steel pipes and helped the oil-rich Middle East urbanize. The rise of economic prosperity, the spread of the city culture and the increased use of energy and hence, of gadgets in all walks of life, even unintentionally, increased steel use among societies across the world. Indeed, the use of steel per capita is often an indication of social and economic development of a country.

Steel is bulky and hence is dependent on freight and becomes largely localized

Steel is bulky; it packs far less value per unit of weight than copper or aluminum or, for that matter, of plastics. If return on investments is considered by tonnage, then steel does not give the best returns. However, steel is produced in large chunks that attract substantial sums of money, and steel may often give better returns on gross bloc when compared to other materials. A mid-sized car consumes about a tonne and a half of steel, and an apartment of 1000 square feet has about a tonne of steel framed into it. Steel, being so commonly used in every walk of life and the sheer bulk of the material, makes it difficult for steel to travel very far. Countries like Japan, that have to import raw materials, namely iron ore and coal, prefer to be located on the sea coast. Japan must pay for the import of its raw materials and hence, must become a net exporter of steel. This explains the high standards and productivity of the Japanese steel industry – for it must make enough money by producing and exporting steel in order to be able to afford to buy the raw materials.

The principle ingredients of steel are iron and carbon, and while iron is sourced from iron ore and carbon from coal, steel is made in the presence of enormous heat. The chemical reactions also require fluxes, namely in the form of limestone and dolomite. A tonne of steel can consume up to four tonnes of raw materials, including coal out of which coke is made and power is generated. Therefore, each tonne of steel involves a cartage of five tonnes of material (four of the raw material and one of the finished steel). Steel, thus, clearly dominates the freight business, ports and warehouses. The ease or the difficulty of transportation underlies many decisions around investments in the steel business, in expanding capacities and choosing the technique of production. For a country like India, where extensive deposits of iron ore help in the setting up of steel plants, steel plants are located around the sources of iron ore. Unfortunately, these areas of deposits of iron ore are located deep inland, and the road to the ports or to the mainland in India is arduous. The choice of location of steel plants near the sources of raw materials might place a cap on the scale of operations and the capacity size of plants, precisely due to problems of logistics. There is always a pay off between locating a plant close to the ports or close to the source of raw materials. Mega steel plants with capacities over 10 million tonnes often choose to be located near sea coasts, rather than near raw materials. A country like India, that has its own deposits of iron ore, may choose to remain a self-sufficient producer of steel. Companies producing steel in India out of captive mines deep inside the forests inland face enormous difficulties in bringing their finished steel to markets in the cities; roads are often too narrow for trailers to carry extra wide sheets. Constraints in roads or railways place limits on the capacities of steel plants, even when they are located close enough to mines.

Steel remains largely a localized industry, dependent on the local availability of raw materials. Japan, which is among the top steelmakers of the world, imports all of it raw material, but not from far. Its iron ore is sourced from India, and coal from Siberia and Manchuria. Similarly, Canada supplies iron ore and coal to the USA. Steel cannot travel far nor can its raw materials be carted easily around the world. The fortunes of the steel industry are equally dependent upon the vagaries and fluctuations in the freight market. The problem of carting steel makes it a localized affair. The oil crisis of 1973 was the beginning of nationalization of the steel industry, when every country realized that freight was the largest component of costs of steel (and smaller countries which did not have large trade connections and did not operate their own vessels often ended up paying huge fares for ships). West Germany, in those days, used bank finances to liberally invest in transportation and logistics, and invested heavily into riverine transport as well.

The complex labour skills deployed in the manufacturing of steel

But, there is yet another reason why steel becomes geographically affixed, and this is skill. Humans are not as mobile as capital and procedures for immigration are often harsh. Education is perhaps the least standardized global product, and few joint ventures exist in knowledge management. Skill shortages appear to be the greatest crisis that the steel industry is set to face. Ranstad CPE, a major recruiter in the UK, supposedly warned the British steel industry that skill shortages may eventually lead to the closure of firms.[4] In Adelaide, the construction of a $24 million superway was cancelled due to skill shortages.[5] Indeed, the repeated downsizing of steel mills, the retrenchments and the layoffs, and pay cuts during downturns, have identified steel as a sunset industry. The new generation entering the workforce no longer looks at the steel industry as a good employer. Producing steel on an industrial scale requires the coming together of many kinds of skills, including those of metallurgy; electrical, mechanical and chemical engineering; knowledge of chemistry and thermodynamics; operations management; logistic experts; automation engineers; and programmers and strategists. The wide array of skills must work together and in a team. When steel plants are shut down and workers retrenched, the society loses a huge skill base, and while the plant and machinery can be relocated elsewhere, skilled persons hardly travel out. Steel plant mechanization and automation has also led to a shrinkage of steel employment and for production of about 1600 million tonnes; the steel industry worldwide employs only 4 million workers. In the case of India, however, the proportion of workers to fixed capital in the steel industry has fallen drastically from 2005–06 to the 2013–14.

Flat steel, long steel

Steel can be in a flat shape, like the plate, or may be a long product in the form of a bar. These sections can be heavy, medium or light. The heavy plates are used for bridges, platforms, oil rigs and ships. The relatively lighter ones are used for railway wagons and the lightest ones are used for automobiles and consumer durables like refrigerators, washing machines and so on. The long products can be used as beams, joists, rails and pillars. The medium and light structures are used for construction of residential buildings, for window and doorframes and for factories and public utility buildings. Steel constitutes 6% of the cost of construction and 12% of the cost of manufacture of consumer goods; no wonder, then, there is a preference among the steel manufacturers to produce flats because of the larger share of value in the final price realization of the finished product. The steel plants which produce flat products are necessarily larger in scale because larger scale is needed when casting and rolling out flat and wide sheets. The steelmakers who wish to enter into the flats market are therefore larger scale producers and usually produce in integrated mills, so that they can keep a tighter control on the consistency of the material. Rolling out flat steels is more sensitive to the consistency of the material because the material is spread out thinner over a larger area; long products are denser per unit surface and much of the non-homogeneity of the metal may be overlooked and tolerated. The production of flat steels and the use of an integrated route to produce steel are thus closely correlated.

Large-scale and small-scale steel – technologies to produce steel

Usually, when steel is produced directly out of iron ore and coke, the latter being a residue of coal from which the volatile matters have been released, one uses the oxygen route. This is also known as the primary route of steelmaking because it uses the natural minerals to make steel. The oxygen route compares with an alternative route of steelmaking, which is the electric route. In the latter, one uses steel scrap or directly reduced iron, or a form of solid iron extracted from the ore. The heat in the oxygen steelmaking route comes from the coke oven gas, while in electric steelmaking it comes from the electricity, charged in the form of an "arc". The oxygen steelmaking route operates in very large scale: the minimum economic size of a basic oxygen furnace (BOF) plant should be anywhere between 3 and 5 million tonnes per annum, while that of the electric arc furnace could be between 0.3 to 3 million tonnes.[6] The cost of raw materials and energy vary between the two processes, and while iron ore is usually cheaper than scrap, the energy requirements in the oxygen route are thrice as much as in the electric furnaces. Metallics constitute 50% of the cost of production in the BOF route, while for the electric arc furnace it is as high as 75%. Energy costs in the electric route are lower than those of the BOF, and the capital costs in the BOF can be as high as $1100 per tonne, while for the electric furnaces these could be as low as $300 per tonne. On the whole, the costs of steelmaking is not remarkably lower in the BOF.

Laplace Consel and Platts assess that steel production through the electric arc furnace is favourable, in many respects, compared to steel produced through the basic oxygen route.[7] The new Greenfield plants in the blast furnace route, also known as the integrated route or basic oxygen furnace route, can cost as high as $800 to $1200 per tonne. In comparison to this, the electric furnaces can be set up at anywhere between $150 and $300 per tonne. The annual maintenance cost is 7% of the CAPEX costs and this means that the maintenance costs of the electric arc furnace, or the EAF are a fraction of that of the oxygen furnaces. Moreover, in the integrated complexes, replacements come in large and indivisible chunks, and the costs of replacements could be daunting. To replace a coke oven costs nearly $400 per tonne. Modernization of the integrated mills could be daunting, and much of the obsolete technology in steel may indeed come in through the electric route. The environmental costs are steep as well, as integrated plants are polluting, while the electric routes are mostly clean. The electric route of steelmaking depends upon steel scrap as its input. Developed countries generate more scrap than developing ones because they have been using steel products for a longer time and many of their old cars, dilapidated flyovers and fatigued machines need scrapping. For developing economies, in which capital is scarce, scrap is scarce as well.

But, India has shown yet another way forward for electric steelmaking to the world and it is most interesting.

India's innovation in electric steelmaking – steel production grows by leaps and bounds

The Indian steel industry expanded by leaps and bounds in the 1980s, on the might of the electric steelmaking route. But the cost of scrap grew steeply on the increased demand for scrap from India, and it was then that the steelmakers in the electric route manipulated the induction furnace for making steel. Just as the electric arc furnace was a fraction of the cost of the integrated steel plant, so the induction furnace was a fraction of the electric arc furnace. But the problem of the electric route has always been its limitation in steel refining; this problem was exacerbated in the induction furnace even deeper. The induction furnace was known as being a garbage in and garbage out technique, and hence, the quality of the billets depended on the quality of the feed material, scrap, in this case.

Sustainability issues in producing steel – financial, resources, skills and environmental

A formidable problem of steel, wherever it is produced, is sustainability. The term sustainability has many connotations. Although its most common reference is climate and the environment, sustainability can mean a host of other things as well, that stand in the way of the smooth running of the business. There are many kinds of sustainability, namely, financial, resource, operational, ecological and environmental. Financial sustainability means that the business must earn minimum profits so that wages can be paid, interest serviced, plant and machinery maintained and raw materials procured. In recent times, the falling prices of finished products and the rising prices of raw materials have seriously threatened the financial sustainability of the steel business. In the industrial age, steel is usually produced on a large scale, with oxygen routes of at least a million tonne per annum and electric routes of at least half a million tonne per annum. Such scales do not permit production to adjust minutely to quantities of demand, and thus, demand is sometimes unmet, and sometimes production is in excess, leading to unsold stocks. Steel capacities that are planned to meet the demand may often take about five to six years to materialize, and if by that time the economic cycle takes a downturn, then the new Greenfield capacities may face market glut. CAPEX remain high and the firms are hurt by depressed prices; such situations may often throw new capacities into the whirlpool of losses from which recovery may be difficult. Steel companies do best when they are matured; their fixed costs are all recovered and the ratio of debt and equity is one or even lower.

Sometimes, countries may lose their raw material resources, like most of the European nations who have exhausted their iron ore and coal deposits; in some countries such as Russia and the United States, skilled workers have retired and aged and even died without being replaced by a younger lot. These are failings of resource sustainability. The most serious problem of steel, is however, its environmental sustainability. Steel emits two times as much carbon as its volume, and ranks among the top polluting industries of the world. Since humanity has to produce steel, management of emissions is a major challenge for the steelmakers. Indeed, management of the environment has become one of the most lucrative businesses of the steel industry. The steel industry tries to ward off this bad name of being environmentally polluting by stating that because steel lasts for at least a quarter century; its long life cycle cost ensures that the environmental impact of steel is minimized. While this may be true for the heavier sections such as joists and beams, and even for the bars and rods used for construction, imaginging that steel in washing machines, automobiles or in airplanes and supermax ships will be made to last that long is not acceptable. The sum and substance of this is that steel does pollute, and the management of emissions and the treatment of effluents are likely to remain of very central concern for the technologists of steel.

Notes

1 Jared Diamond. *Guns, Germs and Steel – The Fates of Human Societies*. New York. WH Norton and Company. 1997, p. 10.
2 Jacob Bronowoski. *The Ascent of Man*. BBC Books. Imprint of Random House. London. 2011, pp. 95-97.
3 Jack Goody. *Metals, Culture and Capitalism – An Essay into The Origins of The Modern World*. Cambridge, UK. Cambridge University Press. 2012, pp. 74-75.
4 http://planningandbuildingcontroltoday.co.uk/hr-skills/steel-crisis-trigger-skills-emergency/23691/
5 http://indaily.com.au/news/local/2016/01/13/superway-build-plagued-by-steel-skills-shortages/
6 www.ceps.eu/system/files/Steel%20Report.pdf (p. 17).
7 Marcel Genet. EAF and/or BF/BOF: Which route is best for Europe? Laplace Conseil and Platts. 2012. www.laplaceconseil.com/LaplaceConseil/htdocs/admin/upload/File/MarcelGenetPlatts1205.pdf

2 Parameters of steel policy in India

Governments across the world usually intervene in the affairs of their respective steel industries precisely because steel consumes huge amounts of resources in terms of money, manpower, electricity, water, land and minerals. Societies must sacrifice significant proportions of their present gratification in order to be able to build up savings for investments into steel businesses. There must be sufficient investments in education for people to be skilled in order for them to run as complex a business as that of steel. Steel uses natural resources like water, land and minerals which are irreplaceable. With such a heavy concentration of resources, steel cannot be left to the vagaries of the market to demolish its capital. Subsidies, protection, promotions and even caps on investments appear in the form of government policies around the steel industry. Since producing steel also means that the producers corner a lion's share of resources of the society, which the production of steel requires, the steel industry creates asymmetries of property, capital and economic power. The indispensability of steel, and yet the unequal command over resources, makes every government desire some form of control or some influence over its steel industry.

Steel in colonial times

The indigenous steel industry started in India in the year 1907 with the setting up of the Tata Iron and Steel Company, or TISCO, by an Indian subject Jamshedji Tata. But much before that, as early as 1830, British civil servants and professionals started experimenting with steel production in India in Bhadravati, Porto Novo and even in the Kumaon Hills. The steelmaking facilities were set up on a trial basis in these areas of the princely states, away from the direct rule of the British. The British subjects who thought of making steel were also in the mood to defy the Empire by developing modern technology. If we place the time of these steel facilities against the fact that it was not before 1856 that Henry Bessmer installed the facility to kick-start modern steelmaking in Britain, one may ask whether the British in India were ahead of those in the home country in ambitions to industrialize. India's steel ambitions are extensions of those dreams.[1]

Steel with the coming of the post-independence planned economy

The Indian industries were controlled through a series of licenses and permits in the form of the *Industries (Development and Regulation) Act of 1951.* The idea of such a system of control was to allow only the very competent producers to invest in steel, so that capital, which was scarce in India at the time as mentioned above, would not be wasted at the hands of entrepreneurs who did not have where-withal to make steel efficiently. This fear makes sense, because if the technology to produce steel, which was not as standardized as it is at present, were to fall in the hands of unqualified persons, it would entail a waste of resources. Indeed, in the 1950s and 1960s the technology to produce steel was indeed difficult to access. The government stepped in to set up large integrated steel plants which could process mineral ores into finished steel in one go. Initially, there were four steel such steel plants, namely Rourkela Steel Plant, Durgapur Steel Plant, Bhilai Steel Plant and Bokaro Steel Plant, that were eventually managed by a holding company, also wholly owned by the government, namely Steel Authority of India, or SAIL.

Smaller producers as supplements to the large integrated plants

The steel sections that were rolled out of the large integrated mills had to be cut into shapes, often rolled out or made into sheets and smaller sections, in order to be fit for use by small local customers. Licenses were devised, in order to allow the setting up of small steel processors who would roll out bars and rods, angles and channels out of the billets cast out by the larger steel plants. In Europe, such processors would typically constitute the steel service centres, but in India, sta-tistically, these processors were counted as steel producing units. The number of units, the capacities of each of these, as well as the exact sections they could roll out, were all planned meticulously through academic exercises before the licenses could be issued. The Joint Plant Committee, hereafter the JPC, a body constituted by the Ministry of Coal, Steel and Mines in 1964, was set up in order to carry out the above exercises.

Not merely capacities: the JPC "fixes" prices as well

Steelmaking, being restricted to only a few producers, raised some uncertainties over the adequacy of supply. As demand increased, due to an increase in the levels of economic activities, and the rise in prosperity of the people, the challenge to increase the supply of steel became important. It was easy for the steel producers to raise the price of steel because there were no competitors. But, the government had strict control over the steel prices. The steel prices were literally "fixed" by the government, which allowed the steel plants to meet their costs with a small markup that would help in reinvesting towards expanding capacities and maintenance of the plant; needless to say, the prices covered the costs of the least efficient steel plant and created neat surpluses for the more efficient plants. While on the one hand, it allowed the less efficient plants to be complacent, it also allowed the more efficient plants to increase their capacities out of the surpluses they had accumulated. No wonder then, that we see steel plants such as Bokaro Steel Limited and Bhilai Steel Plant grow, while Durgapur Steel Plant and Rourkela Steel Plants have been much slower to accumulate capacities. Pricing of steel products was the cornerstone of policy around steel in India. Here again, the Joint Plant Committee played a commendable role.

Government creates funds for investments in steel

By the year 1978, the Government had created two levies, namely the Steel Development Fund, which could be as high as 25% of the market prices of steel, and a Rs 3 to Rs 5 per tonne of steel sold as the JPC Cess. The latter, would take care of the establishment costs of the Joint Plant Committee and the Steel Development Fund, or the SDF would constitute a kitty, out of which to fund the modernization programmes of the steel plants. Both funds were managed by the Ministry of Steel. As a result of this, the modernization programmes as well as the activities of the JPC, mainly in working out the product mix and fair prices, were well coordinated and industrial synergies between the large plants and the smaller ones as well as among the plants themselves were worked out quite well. The supply side was well coordinated and well adjusted to market conditions. All through the 1970s and the 1980s oversupply was never an issue.

Freight equalization scheme

The Government of India was very clear that steel had to reach every part of the country as part of its agenda of balanced development. The idea of balanced development means that every geographical region of the country should develop equally, and for this steel would need to be available equally across the land. But steel plants were concentrated in the east, and the high costs of transport would have unfairly increased the prices of steel in the rest of the country. In order to flatten out the variations in freight, the consumers in the east paid more per kilometer, in order to subsidize the consumers in the rest of the country. The control of freight was yet another major pillar of the government policy. The three pillars of government policy were thus capacity control, product mix planning and freight equalization. The Freight Equalization Scheme was introduced as early as 1952 as a supplement to the industrial licenses.

Import substitution, export promotion

The focus of the state during the times of control lay in both restricting the production of steel and yet promoting it: restricting, because resources were scarce, and promoting it at the same time because India needed to produce its own steel, if only to be spared of spending valuable foreign exchange on imports. Besides, the production of steel was also looked upon as a means of achieving technological capabilities and economic self-reliance. Importance was attached on the import of technology, of machinery and even inputs, such as coking coal, and in order to be able to pay for such imports, exports were also encouraged. The duty drawback scheme incentivized exports, by allowing producers to claim back the duties paid on imported inputs (used for the manufacture of exports).

State control over industry annulled, industry rediscovers the role of the state: national steel policy 2005

After 1991, however, the Indian economy was liberalized, and state control was lifted. The plants, including those in the private sector, were free to take decisions of how much to produce, what to produce, for who to produce, when to produce and through which means to produce. Government control over the steel industry was annulled and no longer was the Ministry of Steel needed to oversee the requirements for licenses and capacities, or to suggest fair prices or to send in notes related to the need for import of raw materials, especially steel scrap. In terms of common sense, the Ministry of Steel and its bodies no longer needed to exist, and soon committees were constituted to euthanize bodies, such as the Joint Plant Committee and the Development Commissioner of Iron and Steel. The latter, was duly dissolved but the former, continued to thrive and in fact grow, to greater importance. The survival of the Joint Plant Committee showed that the role of the state was far from being over, even after controls on the industry lifted. The industry, as it appeared, needed the state even more, after delicensing and decontrol and the role of the state changed from that of a controller into a facilitator for the industry. The change in the role of the state was expressed through the National Steel Policy of 2005.

The eagerness with which the industry welcomed the National Steel Policy of 2005, revealed that the role of the State was indeed desired rather than being resented. Far from the industry dispensing with the state, they looked upon the institution to provide a direction to the economy, on the whole. Papers were churned out on how much steel the industry needed to produce, and in what kind of product: mix, light, medium or heavy and long or flats. The Joint Plant Committee calculated the overall demand for steel, as well as gave a sectoral breakup of the construction sector, rural areas, infrastructure needs and so on. A target of 300 million tonnes of steel was thus set to be accomplished by the year 2020, and surely a flurry of MoUs and letters of intent were signed up between the promoters and state governments to put up steel plants. The demand projections had to be revised many times, and soon, in one of its revisions, the demand forecast was halved to 140 million tonnes by 2019-20. Presently, there is a further downward revision to 110 million tonnes.

The focus of the National Steel Policy of 2005 was to enhance the production of steel, because it was felt that the demand for steel in India could only gallop in times to come (with industrialization, urbanization and improvements in transport and wireless connectivity). Almost every question raised in the Indian Parliament around the steel industry was centred on whether the production of steel in India is increasing or not, as if the unfettered expansion in production and production capacities can be a well-justified ends in themselves. Once the target of increased production is unquestioned, the steel policy ties up with a raw material policy, on the one hand, and trade protection policy on the other.

Mineral policy becomes important for a liberalized industry

Having projected a gargantuan volume of 300 million tonnes of steel, albeit revised down to only about a 110 million tonnes annually by 2019–20, the challenge of the Ministry was to ensure the availability of iron ore. Assuming that a tonne of steel requires about 1.6 tonnes of iron ore, 300 million tonnes would require about 480 million tonnes of iron ore. Given that India's reserves are 28 billion tonnes, iron ore can said to last only for about half a century more, only if there is no growth in steel production beyond 300 million tonnes. Coal might last longer, to perhaps some sixty years. Steel production consumes huge amounts of water, and given the shortage of water in India, especially in the iron-rich states of Karnataka, Maharashtra, Andhra Pradesh and parts of Odisha, water could emerge as a major scarcity. Thousands of millions of Indian rupees need to be invested in laying railway tracks, renovating ports and producing electricity, to be able to support steelmaking capacities of such gigantic proportions. The above, could involve reaching different levels of investments altogether.

The raw material policy of the Indian steel industry is based upon three pillars. Firstly, the acquisition of new mines, both within India as well as abroad, in which issues of land acquisition, environmental clearances and compensation (to the communities displaced as a result of mineral explorations) are addressed. Secondly, there is a move to use more of the available stock of iron ore through beneficiation and pelletization. Thirdly, there is encouragement to augment domestic supplies of iron ore through the imposition of tax on exports of iron ore.

Government moves to protect steelmaking capacities

We have mentioned how the Indians revel in an endless increase in the production of steel, and with the excess steelmaking capacities across the world, and consequently the threat of cheap imports, the policy makers are also concerned with the protection of domestic steel production and capacities. Unfortunately, for the steel industry in India, the policy makers are biased against the electric steel producers, and regard steel produced through the oxygen route as the legitimate source of steel production. The Quality Control Orders, since 2007, try to protect the steel made through the oxygen route against the steel made through the electric route. The Quality Control Orders openly forbid the production of steel of poor quality, and indeed, in the earlier orders steel produced in the electric furnaces, were assumed to be of poor quality. In India, only steel produced in the blast furnaces could qualify for government tenders in projects. Very recently, the route of steelmaking has been relaxed, but the quality norms are rather stringent, notwithstanding the fact that the quality of steel which a high-rise apartment needs, may be very different from what an ordinary construction of a village shed may need. By nearly banning the production of steel of lower grades, the Quality Control Orders run the risk of retarding a wider consumption of steel, especially in the rural areas (where steel pipes as pillars, steel sheets of roofing material and steel wire mesh as chicken pen may all shift to plastics and polythene).

In a way then, the Quality Control Orders contradict the policy of promoting the consumption of steel, especially in rural India. The per capita consumption of steel in India, at just 60 kgs per annum, is very low by global standards, and this makes India a steel poor country, despite it being the third largest steel producing country in the world. In view of this anomaly, policy makers have persistently pursued the case of promoting steel consumption in rural India. The Institute for Steel Development and Growth, or INSDAG, has been specifically set up for this purpose. The quality of steel that needs to be produced for rudimentary rural uses, need not be of a similar quality required in flyovers and railway tracks, or in ships and high-rise apartment homes; the Quality Control Order deters the grades of steel produced for the ruder uses by the village fabricators.

The Minimum Import Price, on imported steel mill products since the middle of 2016, by making steel prices in India steep, and guarding imports by price barriers, may have the effect of shifting the metal product and fabrication industry out of the country. Indeed, the slogan of Make in India may be severely affected in view of higher steel prices, as steel-using downstream industries are likely to shift out of the country. Protectionist measures may deter the downstream industries, while protecting the domestic industry. Besides, one cannot overlook the fact that only a less efficient industry needs protection against imports, and thus, protectionism for steel in India is also accompanied by yet another set of policies that pertain to the competitiveness for Indian steel. Policies designed towards improving competitiveness for the Indian steel industry incurves upon the availability of cheap raw materials, subsidized power, easy loans and tax holidays, in other words, the very components of the infant industry.

The Government of India also actively promotes exports of all commodities and steel, gets the benefits of such export promotion measures as well. Under the new Foreign Trade Policy, credit slips are provided for small producers to settle taxes, and duties only after the merchandise trade has been concluded, duties may be drawn back on exported items, duty-free inputs for exports may be obtained and technology in the form of machinery and software may be imported free of cost. The crux of export promotion is then, credit and waivers on the inputs required for exports.

Understanding new ways of doing business in steel

The policies of government are, in essence, seeking to maintain the sanctity of production; however, exports protect production by creating a demand for steel offshore. Protection of the domestic markets against imports, and the insistence on investments in infrastructure, so that domestic players are as well positioned as the global players, are also ways of defending productive capacities. But in the free market for steel, the verdict is clear, which is that there is excess capacity. Countries are devising myriad ways to get around the problem, by collaborating across steel firms within, as well as outside the country. Austria, Canada, Norway and much of Europe, is slowly dividing and reintegrating the integrated steel producers, and a slew of electric furnaces, so that they can approach the steel market in complementary ways, in terms of mild steel and alloy steel, steel mill products, steel tool and component markets and so on. In fact, the countries of the EU have divided up the space among them; with England, France, Italy, Belgium and Netherlands focusing on mild steel while Austria, Luxembourg, Switzerland and others specialize in alloy steel products. Production sharing is yet another strategy in which China invests in Africa and South America; buys minerals from the countries of these continents; produces in these very countries and sells locally. The Japanese steel industry has invested in India, into Nippon Denro, JSW, Tata Steel and Bhushan Steel, in order to procure material for the automobile companies that they have located in India, an instances of new strategies of production sharing. Intra-industry investments are also strategies of globalization (with a view to work within excess capacities). An instance of intra-industry specialization may be investors from Belgium and the Netherlands, who take care of Luxembourg's needs for mild steel, while developing capacities in it for the manufacture of engineering goods, machinery and components.

The above, are the instances of how firms operate globally through trade and investments, in order to manage overcapacity that has accrued worldwide.

A McKenzie report of 2002, by Etienne Denoel et al., titled, "Saving Steel: The World Has Too Much Steelmaking Capacity, But Tariffs Are Not the Answer",[2] mentions clearly that the world is pathetically stuffed with excess capacity, and that the only way to emerge out of this situation is to have another steel company dedicated towards the management of this capacity. The author suggests that the excess capacities may be addressed through cross-border collaborations in production and steel processing; the excess production in some items of steel may be traded against the excess production in some others, and surplus steel may be sourced from elsewhere to fabricate steel products for both the domestic markets as well as for exports.

Notes

1   Manohar Bandopadhyay. *The Story of Public Sector Steel*. Publication Division. Government of India. 1987, pp. 13-16.
2   Etienne Denoel, I., Sigurd Mareels and Simon Winter; "Saving Steel: The World Has Too Much Steelmaking Capacity, but Tariffs Are Not the Answer." *The McKinsey Quarterly*. www.questia.com/library/jpurnal/1G1-90701261/saving-steel-the-world-has-too-much-steelmaking-capacity

3 Excess capacity and production of steel in the world

The problem of the steel industry today lies in worldwide overproduction; it appears that the world needs no more steel than what it already consumes. In 2014, the world produced a million tonnes of steel more than it consumed, but on the whole, the world used no more than 75% of its installed capacity. This means that 550 million tonnes of capacity is left unutilized, out of the 1650 million tonnes that was produced that year. With a slight increase in the demand for steel, the idle capacities can suddenly awaken and swing into action. The overcapacity of steel is the key to the problem of the steel industry at present. To many observers and economists, this may sound strange, for is not steel the material of the modern world? Does it not lie at the core of every activity of modern industries, in the form of machines, tools, gadgets, buildings, infrastructure and transport? Is not steel the marrow of the body economic, the largest connective tissue of industrial development? Then, is not the overcapacity in steel only a temporary affair, soon to be mitigated with the rise in demand for steel? Is it not naïve to imagine that what is only a temporary affair will last into the steady state of the future? The present chapter will address exactly these questions and discuss why overcapacity is here to stay and translate into a persistent, if not defining feature of the steel industry.

Is excess capacity in the steel industry here to stay?
Yes, because the world has too much stuff

The overproduction of steel is aligned to a general overproduction in all commodities. John Kenneth Galbraith has discussed the problem of overproduction of commodities brilliantly in his book, *The Affluent Society*.[1] Of course, one may find new demand, if we discover new stuff, but with the array of goods and commodities at our disposal, we are clearly headed towards what we may call "Stuffocation", a symptom that James Wallman discusses in his latest book by the same name.[2] More stuff worries us, and the more we invest to produce stuff that suffocates us, the lower the price we may expect our consumers to pay. More stuff means more raw materials, and if these raw materials consist of the irreplaceable minerals of the earth, fixed in supply in nature, the prices of inputs are going to rise. Falling product prices and rising costs of production are squeezing manufacturing profits everywhere. This is the situation in which India looks towards producing 300 million tonnes of steel, albeit a decade hence from now.

State of overcapacity in the world steel industry: not so much excess production as much as excess capacity

Table 3.1 shows global crude steel production volumes and capacity figures – as assessed by World Steel Association and by the OECD – and the resulting calculation of steelmaking capacity utilization. Excess capacity seems to grow progressively, and in 2017 the global excess of world steel capacity is expected to increase to approximately 807 million tonnes.[3]

Between 2004 and 2013, the global production of steel increased by 586 million tonnes, while consumption increased only slightly less, by 585 million tonnes, bringing the problem of excess steel production to only a million tonnes. There may not be a significant overproduction in terms of unsold tonnage, but the problem lies in the excess capacity in plants. There may be pockets in the world in which steel is in short supply, and there are countries for which steel is in excess supply. Since steel is a bulk commodity that is heavy to carry and freight rates are rising by the day, steel cannot flow that easily across regions, which makes a country install its own steelmaking capacity, rather than to source this heavy material from abroad. Besides, steel is too important a material, too basic for the modern lifestyle, not to be self-sufficient in. Such mentalities around the self-sufficiency in steel have created what we see as overcapacity.

The production of steel for the world as a whole has increased by 586 million tonnes in a span of a decade, and when compared with a base figure of a billion tonne of steel in 2004, it is evident that the growth of steel production has been at an average rate of 5% per annum. But when we look at the decomposed figure for the regions (Table 3.2), we observe that steel production has dropped violently in the European Union, substantially in North America, significantly in the CIS countries and in Australia and somewhat in Africa as well. But Asia, comprising mainly of

Table 3.1 Steel production and steelmaking capacity in the world

	In million tonnes		
Year	*Production*	*Capacity*	*Excess capacity*
2012	1560	2102	542
2013	1650	2273	623
2014	1670	2322	652
2015	1622	2371	749
2016	1608	2402	794
2017	1615	2422	807

Source: www.steelonthenet.com

India and China and the Middle East to an extent, has increased the production of steel. Interestingly steel production has also increased in non-EU Europe. The data in Table 3.2 suggests a geographical relocation, if not a concentration of steelmaking facilities in Asia.

Let us turn to the pattern of steel consumption across the regions of the world presented in Table 3.3.

Table 3.2 Regionwise global production of crude steel

Region	2004	2014	Change
	In thousand tonnes		
European Union	202523	166208	−36315
Other Europe	23992	38762	14770
CIS	113363	108256	−5107
North America	134021	118942	−15079
South America	45875	45822	−53
Africa	16706	16078	−628
Middle East	14253	26967	12714
Asia	503508	1122680	619172
Oceania	8300	5588	−2712
World	1062541	1649303	586762

Source: Steel Statistics Year Book, 2014.

Table 3.3 Regionwise global use of steel in crude steel equivalent

Region	2004	2014	Change
	In thousand tonnes		
European Union	189265	153286	−35979
Other Europe	24672	39945	15273
CIS	44905	67055	22150
North America	172548	149014	−23534
South America	34470	51556	17086
Africa	19820	36783	16963
Middle East	32320	55065	22745
Asia	535580	1087902	552322
Oceania	8815	7520	−1295
World	1062396	1648126	585730

Source: Ibid.

Consumption appears to have contracted in the EU, North America and Oceania regions, while for the rest of the world, consumption of steel has increased. Of course, Asia tops the chart, driving the growth in consumption. No less is the rise in steel use, in the CIS and the Middle East. South America and Africa, too, appear to have a good hunger for steel.

Comparing the production with consumption and subtracting the latter from the former (Table 3.4), we get the excess production of steel. As expected, there is excess production of steel in the EU, North America and CIS and there is steel

Table 3.4 Excess production of global steel in relation to consumption

Excess steel production = Production less steel use (in thousand tonnes)			
Region	*2004*	*2014*	*Remarks*
European Union	13258	12922	Slight mitigation due to the implementation of action plan
Other Europe	−680	−1183	Could do with more capacity
CIS	68458	41201	Mitigation of excess capacities due to migration of countries from CIS to EU
North America	−38527	−30072	Capacity pulled down but use declining faster
South America	11405	5734	Increase in consumption. Good place for relocation from North America
Africa	−3114	−20705	Demand unmet by production
Middle East	−18067	−28098	Rising steel demand
Asia	−32072	34778	Excess consumption now turned into excess production
Oceania	−515	−1932	Rise in consumption but would rely on imports
World	145	1177	Overall excess

Source: Ibid.

appetite to be filled in South America, non-EU Europe, Africa and the Middle East, but the biggest culprit in excess production is Asia. One may expect the EU, North America and the CIS to be exporting robustly to non-EU Europe, to South America and to the Middle East and Africa, but China's excess steel production, despite a strong demand locally, creates a strong presence of exports.

EU, CIS and Asia are pockets of excess supplies, while the Americas and Africa, Oceania and the Middle East, are areas of supply deficits. One would thus imagine that steel will flow from the regions of steel surplus into regions of steel deficits. In Table 3.5, we observe that steel flows from Asia into the NAFTA region, and from EU and CIS into Africa, and from CIS into the Middle East, while Oceania sources steel almost exclusively from Japan, into which it exports its minerals as well. The CIS is rising as a major mineral supplier to the Middle East, while Africa supplies minerals to the EU countries. Most of the trade of China, EU and of the CIS nations takes place within their own region and continents. Steel, thus, does not travel very far, which is why excess capacities are often difficult to relocate (in terms of physical plant and machinery, though investments can flow in and set up steel facilities in the country in which exports are targeted). The mobility of finance capital and the immobility of physical capital causes the overcapacity of steel.

Excess production of steel vs. requirement of steel for products: direct and indirect steel

Steel is an intermediate product used for the manufacture of other products; steel is an input for manufacture of goods. The demand for steel (and the justification for producing it) depends on the manufacture of steel using goods. It may well be possible that steel for the manufacture of automobiles or for machinery takes place entirely with imported steel, and it is just as possible, that nations that produce steel such as India may take to large-scale imports of steel-containing products. The steel-containing products are known as indirect steel. Since indirect steel involves a higher level of sophistication and value addition, it is better for economies to have fabrication facilities than merely steelmaking facilities; rather than steel; the levels of indirect steel production might do well as an indicator of economic development and potential for sustained growth.

In Table 3.5, a rather interesting picture emerges. The indirect exports of steel in the EU exceed its excess production in steel, and this makes the EU into a net importer of steel, albeit of indirect steel, despite excess production of steel. Non-EU Europe may be a net importer of steel, but it imports most of its indirect steel as well, making this region into a very active importer. CIS appears to have excess steel, but given its huge imports of indirect steel in the form of steel products, its fabrication and machine building industry may need rebuilding. North America is a hectic exporter of indirect steel, and so is Asia; both the USA and China export finished steel as well as steel products. North America and Asia are thus poised to lead in the growth of the steel industry precisely, because of their fabrication and steel processing activities. The rest of the world may well be importers of indirect steel, which will create reasons to shut more capacity down.

Table 3.5 Global excess production of steel and indirect exports of steel

Region	Excess steel production = Production less steel use		Remarks	Indirect exports of steel		Remarks
	2004	2014		2004	2014	
	In thousand tonnes			In thousand tonnes		
European Union	13258	12922	Slight mitigation implementation of action plan	4253	16599	Really giving importance to steel service and metal industry
Other Europe	−680	−1183	Could do with more capacity	409	−1343	Importing steel for use of final products made of steel. Good place to invest in integrated mills
CIS	68458	41201	Mitigation of excess capacities	−1481	−11235	Imports steel products. Good place to set up service centres. Steel surplus intensified.
North America	−38527	−30072	Capacity pulled down but use declining faster	−18134	20695	Exports steel products, which keeps steel production up
South America	11405	−5734	Increase in consumption. Good place for relocation from North America	−132	−8577	Importing steel products in large quantities. Good place to set up service centres as well as steel units
Africa	−3114	−20705	Demand unmet by production	−1140	−3978	Good place for service centres and steel mills.
Middle East	−18067	−28098	Rising steel demand	−3358	−7937	Good opportunity for integrated steel complexes
Asia	−32072	34778	Excess consumption now turned into excess production	42339	86336	Enters into direct competition with the US in steel exports
Oceania	−515	−1932	Rise in consumption but would rely on imports	−1874	−5389	Will import steel and steel products
World	145	1177	Overall excess	20882	85171	Exports increased to mitigate surplus

Source: Steel Statistics Year Book, 2014 and own calculations.

Closing in of continents

It is very clear that the Europe, between the EU and the non-EU countries, has created a compact zone of steel production and fabrication. The "Other Europe", comprised of non-EU regions, such as Scandinavia, the Balkans, erstwhile Soviet Union countries and Turkey, have traditionally been the hub of excellent engineering activities. The region, presently, has developed steel hunger precisely, since it is concentrating hard on developing excellence in engineering products and other specialized steel products – especially the heavy sections for construction directed mainly at exports. The countries of this region source steel from both the EU as well as from the CIS countries. With steel production dropping in both the EU and the CIS, and a rise in the indirect exports of steel, it seems that there is an interregional specialization in steel production. The traditional steel producing countries of the EU are producing the steel mill products, while the non-EU countries of Europe are focussing on steel using industries and fabrication. Indeed, Bulgaria, Croatia and Serbia may source their entire consumption of steel from Poland, Luxembourg, the Ukraine and Lithuania. Georgia appears to be totally dependent on the Ukraine for its steel and so is Azerbaijan. Belarus concentrates only on steel sourced from Romania. Steel for Europe has become a matter for international specialization. Investors in non-EU Europe are focused on warehousing, logistics and packaging. Investors in Luxembourg are interested in investing in companies, which procure steel and supplies from across countries and export these to other parts of the world.

The Americas are getting integrated fairly between surpluses and deficits in production within the two continents. The USA supplies steel to Canada, Mexico and to countries of South America. But, the USA is among the top steel-producing countries of the world. It used to produce 60% of the world steel, at the close of the World War II; and, hence, it is sentimental about closing down its steel making capacities. The USA has to go on producing steel, and must export more than what the rest of North America and the whole of South America can absorb.

Soon steel may only be exported as project goods

A good market for USA steel is the Middle East, Africa and Australia. Unfortunately, it is here that the USA enters into tough competition with China. China, which produces half of the global steel, is straddling the world, looking desperately for spaces to offload its huge surpluses. Since China has invested heavily into real estate, infrastructure and mining sector of these countries, it has huge currency reserves with these nations which are then used to import Chinese steel. The USA has yet to work in such a concerted manner as China. The Middle East steel market shows that steel follows investments; if one wants to export steel, then one must invest in projects in that country. China and the USA also clash in Oceania, comprised of Australia and New Zealand. This region is close to the USA and Canada, and now has almost "sold" itself to China because of the Chinese investors in its mineral sector. Who manages to export steel will depend upon who gets to invest more into the "projects".

Postscript: How are the top steel-producing countries faring?

A brief perusal of the top ten steel-producing countries of the world reveal a similar picture. Presented in Table 3.6 are data pertaining to production, which is in excess of steel consumption among the top ten steel producing countries.

By Table 3.6, potential exporters are all the top steel producing countries, except the USA and India. Interestingly, both these countries top the charts in the imposition of trade protectionist measures, which seem to be anomalous, given the fact that they are really not in glut. However, relative growths in production and consumption may reveal a very different picture when India and the USA may turn to markets that, after all, may need protection against imports, if only to prevent a supply glut.

From Table 3.7, we see three kinds of developments in the last decade. India, China and South Korea have expanded steel production above the expansions in consumption, leaving these countries with a steel glut. These countries may export aggressively or defend their domestic market turf. Russia has added some steelmaking capacity but has expanded its steel consumption rather rapidly, while Germany has pulled down capacities despite an increase in consumption. These developments make Russia and Germany attractive destinations for steel exports. Japan, Italy, Spain and the USA are pulling down steel production and reducing steel consumption at even faster rates; as far as steel is concerned, these countries are avoidable destinations for exports.

Table 3.6 Excess production of steel in the top 10 steelmaking countries in the world

	Excess Production	
In thousand tonnes	*2004*	*2013*
China	−14514	50261
Japan	32218	39695
India	−6594	−132
Russia	33909	19113
South Korea	−1579	12142
Ukraine	32160	26420
USA	−28141	−19422
Germany	7811	1145
Italy	−6596	1036
Spain	−5486	2915

Source: Steel Statistical Yearbook, 2015 and own calculations.

Table 3.7 Production, consumption and excess production by the top 10 countries of the world (in thousand tonnes)

	Production of steel			Consumption of steel			Excess production	
	2004	*2013*	*Change*	*2004*	*2013*	*Change*	*2004*	*2013*
China	272798	821990	549192	287312	771729	484417	−14514	50261
Japan	112718	110595	−2123	80500	70900	−9600	32218	39695
India	32626	81299	48673	39220	81431	42211	−6594	−132
Russia	65583	68856	3273	31674	49743	18069	33909	19113
South Korea	47521	66061	18540	49100	53919	4819	−1579	12142
Ukraine	38733	32771	−5962	6573	6351	−222	32160	26420
USA	99681	86878	−12803	127822	106300	−21522	−28141	−19422
Germany	46374	42645	−3729	38563	41500	2937	7811	1145
Italy	28604	24080	−4524	35200	23044	−12156	−6596	1036
Spain	17621	14252	−3369	23107	11337	−11770	−5486	2915

Source: Steel Statistics Yearbook, 2014.

Conclusion

The world steel industry suffers from overcapacity; more steel is being produced or can be produced than what the world can absorb. The data discussed above communicates that the overcapacity emerges under two conditions: when capacities are set up faster than the growth in demand, or when consumption shrinks faster than the cutback in steelmaking capacities. Unfortunately, we do not have a scenario in which consumption grows and production does not, or when consumption falls and production does not. Usually, production and consumption move together, one or the other being faster than the other. Ways to address overcapacity have indeed, been exports, but exports have usually also accompanied a specialization – in which some countries are left to specialize in steelmaking, and some other choose to specialize in steel products; there is usually trade among these countries. We observe the formation of trade loops where the EU largely trades among themselves, the Americas trade between the North and the South, CIS and the Middle East form a loop, China and Africa and Asia are in a loop and Japan and Australia constitute yet another loop. Steel exports usually follow investments in manufacturing, mining and infrastructure projects and this makes steel a subsidiary of the overall global investment trends.

Notes

1 John Kenneth Galbraith. *The Affluent Society*. Penguin. UK. 1998, pp. 94–95.
2 James Wallman. *Stuffocation – Living More with Less* . Penguin. UK. 2014, p. 17.
3 www.steelonthenet.com/files/metallurgical_coal.html

4 Overcapacity in the Indian steel industry

Madam, it was a really great pleasure meeting with you at STEEL GLOBAL 2016 at Ahmedabad on 10 June 2016. It was really fascinating and encouraging speech by you for secondary producer like us, the knowledge and experience of you in the steel industry is really commendable.

I would like to briefly remind you about us. We are presently running an ERW Pipes & Tubes Plant in Bangalore with installed capacity of 10000 MT; it is really a tough time for Pipes & Tubes manufacturer like us, because of raw material cost. We are buying HR coils from SAIL/JSW/TATA presently; after MIP, they became dictator of the price, as there was no scope of competition from global suppliers. Because of this our production cost went up, and we are unable to compete with the manufactures Mandi Govind Garh & Raipur who are in-house manufacturing their raw materials (Skelp).

Now the question is of our survival, and for this we have decided to invest in an in-house solution for raw materials, and looking for support and assistance from various Govt Depts for setting up a small steel plant, which has the facility to convert molten steel into narrow width HR coils, complaining with all parameters to sustain competition.

Madam, I am seeking your advice on the same and asking if your department can give us any support or assistance in achieving the objective as mentioned above. Madam, I have a belief that you can help us on the same and guide accordingly. In case it is required I can come to your office to meet you on the same.

Surya Prakash, Shivaferric. 12 June 2016.

Overcapacity: a loss of synergy?

The above letter is self-explanatory; for in it lies the hidden script of why the Indian steel industry, despite a healthy growth in demand, nonetheless, has a tendency to accumulate fat. The reason is simple: there is noncooperation among the large and the small producers of steel. The large integrated steel plants wish to expand their capacities not only for the manufacture of crude steel, but also for the steel mill products. Conventionally in India, during the period between 1940 and 1980, the large integrated plants would manufacture semis, while the secondary, stand-alone and fractal facilities, would roll out to narrower sections, known generally as the steel mill products. But since the 1980s as the integrated steel plants, mainly SAIL and

Tata Steel, expanded their capacities, they stepped into downstream mill products. A possible reason for the extension into the steel mill products was, perhaps, the decision to manufacture wide and extra deep drawn flat hot rolled sheets and coils, which so far, had been imported from abroad. The step into the production of hot rolled flat products marked a new regime of relations between the integrated steel-makers and the downstream producers; the former were no longer interested in supplying semis to the secondary standalone facilities. By the 1980s, these rerollers started setting up smaller electric furnaces to make their own steel, much like the writer of the letter quoted above, who emerged in the market to make only ten thousand tonnes of ERW pipes, and now, had to set up an induction furnace to manufacture that much steel and then skelp. The production of pipes immediately added that much crude steel capacity.

Not cheap imports but excess production is the reason behind the glut in India

As per the data from JPC in 2016, India produced 92 million tonnes of steel including alloy steels and net of interplant transfer for "own consumption" or semis absorbed in the process of production of downstream products by the same firm. Against this, the consumption of steel was only 77 million tonnes, leaving us with a surplus production of 15 million tonnes. The imports during the same year were about 9 million tonnes and exports roughly 6 million tonnes, leaving us with a net import of 3 million tonnes leaving India with a total 18 million tonnes of excess supply. Obviously, imports are far less of a factor in creating a glut in the market; overproduction by domestic producers is the culprit.

The scenario has been presented in Table 4.1. It clearly shows that the export of semis, instead of channelizing these for the domestic downstream producers, has resulted in a surge in imports, and hence, eventually, to a supply glut. First there is a loss of synergy, and then, a surge in imports and the miscalculation between the two creates the excess supply. Were the semis not exported but made available for the domestic downstream processors, there would have been no need for the dupli-cation of steelmaking capacities.

Excess capacities among the steelmakers

We observe in Table 4.2 that only RSP has excess capacity among the public sector steel plants. Among the private sector large integrated mills, namely Tata Steel, JSW, JSPL and Essar Steel, the capacity addition leading to excess bulge is 8.5 million tonnes. The electric arc furnaces add another 6 million tonnes, and the induction furnaces add another 5 million tonnes. Interestingly, it is the electric arc furnaces, consisting of com-panies like Jaiprakash Steel, Punj Llyod, GVK Steel, Lanco Steel and Bhushan Steel, which have scandalously piled up the non-performing assets of the nationalized banks.

On 25 March 2016, *Times of India* reported that Rs 50,000 crores of loans to the steel industry were on the anvil of turning bad.[1] Nearly a year ago, the RBI had issued a warning that five out of the ten top private steel producing companies

Table 4.1 Assessment of market glut in India in 2014–15 (in thousand tonnes)

Products	Production for sale	Consumption	Excess supply	Exports	Mitigation through exports net surplus supply	Imports	Glut due to imports	% of glut to production for sale
Semis	43642	43451	191	640	−449	696	247	1
Bars and rods	32251	31081	1170	392	778	854	1632	5
Structurals	7495	7301	194	83	111	53	164	2
Railway materials	835	851	−16	3	−19	15	−4	0
Plates	4700	4770	−70	559	−629	732	103	2
HR coils/strip	20205	20543	−338	1320	−1658	2006	348	2
HR sheets	1138	1113	25	55	−30	79	49	4
CR coils	7509	8526	−1017	585	−1602	1713	111	1
GP/GC sheets	6892	5554	1338	1629	−291	444	153	2

Source: Own calculations; data is from JPC, 2016.

Table 4.2 Excess capacity among the steel producers in India

Producer	Capacity addition between 2010-11 and 2014-15	Capacity utilization	Excess capacity = capacity addition × capacity utilization
	In thousand tonnes	*In percentage*	*In thousand tonnes*
Bhilai Steel Plant	0	130.85	0
Durgapur Steel Plant	0	112.04	0
Rourkela Steel Plant	2500	52.07	1302
Bokaro Steel Plant	0	86.61	0
IISCO Steel Plant	0	25.40	0
Alloy Steel Plant	0	52.14	0
Salem Steel Plant	180	50.56	91
Visweswaraya Steel Limited	0	11.02	0
Total SAIL	2680	87.47	2344
RINL	0	113.26	0
Total Public Sector	2680	91.55	2453
Private sector			
Tata Steel	2800	97.20	2722
Essar Steel	3940	33.42	1317
JSW	3400	89.97	3059
JSPL	1600	88.93	1423
Other EAF Units	6515	91.98	5992
Corex-BOF MBF-EOF/IF	6553	76.87	5037
Total Private Sector	24808	80.26	19912

Source: JPC, 2016 and own calculations.

could turn into loss-making mammoths. The bad assets of banks, due to the exposure to the steel industry, constitute more than 10 percent of all bad assets, while the total exposure of steel to all loans is about 4.5%. Along with power, steel is one of the worst performing industries in India.[2] The factor responsible for the collapse of steel has been assigned to China, whose huge excess capacity of steel produces close to 50% of all the steel and flushes it across the world, flooding the markets with excess supplies and collapsing prices. Unfortunately the exercises in Table 4.1 of this chapter reveals that, not imports, but excess production, creates the glut in the Indian market.

We know that in the Indian markets, we have 18 million tonnes of excess supply, including net imports, and nearly 20 million tonnes of capacity has been added in excess in the private sector. The public sector has added no more than 2.5 million tonnes of excess capacity, which is acceptable because steel capacities are bulky and cannot be minutely adjusted to the demand. Therefore, the private sector has to be blamed for the excess capacity built up. Of these, JSW and Tata Steel appear to be the worst offenders, each having accumulated to the tune of 3 million tonnes, which is exactly the quantity of net imports. Therefore, it is largely in the interest of Tata Steel and JSW that imports are being curbed through protectionist measures, such as anti-dumping duties, safeguard duties and recently, the imposition of Minimum Import Prices.

Possible reasons for excess production

Import substitution

Excess capacities in the steel industry can emerge due to a variety of reasons, but among the most common reasons are import substitution and anticipation of higher demand in the future. OECD Paper Number 18 from 2014 on global excess capacity notes that excess capacities often emerge during times of demand downturns and are often found to emerge in economies which are net importers of steel. Excess capacity, the paper states, is often an outcome of government intervention in the economy, the award of subsidies and its sensitivity towards retrenchment of labour and job losses.[3] Indeed, the Indian steel companies substitute imports with enthusiasm, not so much out of a desire to match the quality products, but to rise into the zone of higher value additions, through substituting imports, especially, because it is usually the higher value added products that are imported into India.

Between then and 2005, MoUs to the tune of 276 million tonnes were proposed in the states of Odisha, Jharkhand, Chhattisgarh and Karnataka. These investments were various; in the oxygen route, electric arc furnaces, Corex routes and even the induction furnace, albeit of larger sizes. These investments were heavily tilted towards the production of flats, which could not be readily produced out of the small furnaces. Since flat steel was usually imported, the impulses towards import substitution saw the setting up of flat steel capacities that needed larger scales of production.

The China syndrome

The production of lower value steel at home and the import of higher value steel from abroad was a common pattern in the Indian steel industry because India was unable to catch up with the developed world in terms of technological sophistication. But with the coming of the new economy in India, and the freeing of foreign investments into the country, the newer plants are now larger, integrated and use state of the art technology. Imports are now direct competitors of the domestic producers and not complementary to the product mix of the country. There has been a creation of markets for imports, with retailers sometimes preferring cheaper Chinese products to the Indian stuff. China exports almost everything that India produces. Japan and South Korea export specialized inputs for their outsourced automobile and consumer durable markets in India, but China exports simply anything and everything. In the year 2015-16, India imported a total of 12 million tonnes of steel, of which more than a quarter consisted of imports from China.[4] China used to be a very large importer of iron ore from India between 2004 and 2013, during which time much of the payments were done back to back against exports of steel from China to India, if only to keep the Indian currency in balance.

But beyond the China syndrome there are issues of timely delivery, consistency of product quality and the sloth of the Indian steelmaker, which makes at least the automobile industry, that runs on rather stringent parameters, place orders abroad. Global traders are more reliable as suppliers of steel.

Overoptimistic projection of demand

The excess capacity in India is due to two major factors: one being an overoptimistic projection of demand of 300 million tonnes per annum by 2015 (now extended to 2025) and the other being the internal competition between the large integrated steel plants and the smaller electric steel making routes. The large integrated players now wish to enter into the very same market segments of the smaller players. The large integrated steel plants, like the JSPL, spend resources in manufacturing narrow cross sections, which can well be produced by smaller plants by the wayside.[5] The large integrated plant that has the wherewithal of producing very high-quality steel simply is not able to produce the quality that the best steel plants produce in the world.[6] Nonetheless, the large plants want to grab an ever larger share of the market and this is perhaps the reason why they invest in larger capacities to overrun the markets.

Firm behaviour to corner greater market share

Sometimes, in times of declining steel prices, steel companies may want to bring in larger volumes of steel to the market so that what is lost in terms of margins is compensated in terms of volumes. Firms compete among themselves to fan out their tentacles across wider market spectrums, play with a more varied product mix and reserve capacities for the production of semis. Larger volumes were thought to award larger shares of the markets, and hence greater pricing power and insurance against recession. What the steelmakers did not anticipate was that were every producer to plan in this way, new capacities would burgeon. This is exactly what happened in the aftermath of the downturn of 2001-2002.

Policy of value addition by mineral-producing states

Besides, the iron ore producing states, like Odisha, Jharkhand and Karnataka, made it a rule that no mineral was to leave their states without adding value, and hence, sponge iron facilities that made use of iron ore were set up in large numbers. An increase in steel capacity was required in order to use the directly reduced iron thus produced or the lump ore thus mined.

Steel MoUs a ploy to get access to natural resources and land?

But the capacities which came up post-2010, when the world faced yet another downturn, were puzzling because by this time, it was fairly well established that globally there was an overcapacity. It is perplexing as to why the plants, especially the large integrated steel plants in the private sector, embarked upon such massive addition of capacity; when India was steadily losing its export markets and at home, and cheaper and better quality steel from China, Japan and South Korea was flowing in with a steady pace. One possible explanation for this could be that the steel facilities were merely a "front" for the access to mineral resources, namely iron ore mines and coal blocks, as well as land and water resources. Land ownership was a collateral for the promoters to access easy bank loans.

The Indian government, in a bid to protect the natural resources of the country, insists on captive mining, which means the end user alone will be able to extract the minerals for use rather than for sale. 2004 was also a year when the prices of raw materials soared and trade in raw materials yielded magnificent margins. The intention to set up steel plants was a covert way of accessing natural resources, especially land assets with mineral deposits and water reserves. The real intent was land; the lesser intent was steel. It was only an afterthought that the large private players used their clout and influence to curb the smaller players and eat into their market shares.

Measures to reduce excess capacities

Countries across the world take measures to rationalize steelmaking capacities when they are in excess. Chinese banks have stopped lending to steel businesses,[7] while the EU has its Steel Action Plan.[8] Both are government-level initiatives to pare down excess capacities. A pertinent problem that confronts the policy makers is whose capacity is it to cut, whose to curb, whose to promote and whose to hold back. The Ministry of Steel in India has strategized that only those steel mills that produce steel quality of a certain level of BIS standards can produce in the country and has effected a Quality Control Order annually, since 2007. Under this order, it is mandatory to certify steel products with the Bureau of Indian Standards, which covered only a few of the steel items produced in the country. The standards covered steel that were applicable for "heavy" uses in buildings, bridges, automobiles and other applications, but not steel that was ordinarily produced for the local suburban or village markets, for the everyday manufacture of air coolers, garden fencing, chicken pens and other similar household uses. The vast segment of steel units engaged in producing for the low-end consumers, especially in the residential construction sector, stood nullified by the Quality Control Order. While the steel produced by the state of the art mills and the makeshift mills of smaller capacities did not compete in the same market, they, together, created demand for electricity and raw materials, such as sponge iron and scrap, non-coking coal and increased the upward pressure on prices of these crucial raw materials. Also, they made steel appear as available in abundance and this created a downward pressure on prices. The Quality Control Orders attempt to eliminate these capacities, especially those producing steel out of induction furnaces.

The other attack on capacities in the steel industry is the Minimum Import Prices imposed on as many as 173 tariff lines. While this appears as a trade protection measure, it is a powerful attack on capacities of those plants that are not integrated and those which use intermediate mill products as their inputs, such as the cold rollers and the galvanizers who use hot rolled coils as their input.

Revision of projected steel capacities in India

In India, there are three projected steelmaking capacities from various agencies, provided in Table 4.3. Realistically, the capacities should be between 110 and 220 million tonnes at the close of 2020.

Conclusion

Can we say that the excess capacities were created in the Indian steel industry due to the mindset of the policy makers for whom it is important for plants to be integrated in its stages of production? The policy makers in India, for some strange reason, also believe that the best way to produce steel is by the oxygen route and are likely to consider the electric furnace a slightly illegitimate way of production. Indian policy makers have avoided looking at the fact that the stand-alone and fragmentary plants are more competitive than the integrated plants, and this has made companies strive to have steelmaking facilities, leading to excess capacities. Since the policy makers have always believed in import substitution and self-reliance in steel production, trade has never been quite used to achieve specialization and eventual management of excess capacity. In the days after liberalization, when

Table 4.3 Projections of steelmaking capacities by 2020 by various agencies

Agency	Projected capacity of steelmaking by 2020 (in million tonnes)
National Steel Policy, Ministry of Steel, 2005	110
New projections by Ministry of Steel, 2012	220
As per the MoUs signed	293

Source: Rajib Maitra, *Steel and Metallurgy*, Vol. 14, No. 10, August 2012, p. 8.

all controls on industrial capacities were lifted, cooperation among the various segments of the industry turned into competition, each trying to invade the other's turf; competition produced overcapacity.

Notes

1   http://timesofindia.indiatimes.com/business/india-business/Steel-loans-worth-50k-cr-may-turn-bad-in-few-months/articleshow/51545264.cms
2   http://articles.economictimes.indiatimes.com/2015-06-26/news/63862357_1_steel-industry-steel-sector-banking-stability-indicator
3   OECD. "Excess Capacity in the Global Steel Industry and the Implications of New Investment Projects", *OECD Science, Technology and Industry Policy Papers*, No. 18, OECD Publishing. 2015. http://dx.doi.org/10.1787/5js65x46nxhj-en.
4   JPC, 2016.
5   TMT means thermomechanically treated bar, which is a process of administering heat and managing the ferric temperature of the long product throughout the rolling. QTB means quenched and tempered bar, which means reheating and then water quenching to attain a uniform temperature after which it is rolled.
6   Interview with country director, Nippon Steel in Delhi.
7   http://en.yibada.com/articles/118497/20160423/chinas-financial-regulators-to-banks-steel-and-coal-zombie-companies-should-not-be-given-financial-aid.htm; and www.scmp.com/news/china/economy/article/1937629/chinas-banks-told-stop-lending-zombie-steel-and-coal-firms. China would also cut 15% of capacity for its State Owned Enterprises in steel, www.chinadailyasia.com/business/2016-07/08/content_15460367.html.
8   High-level Round Table on the future of the European Steel Industry Recommendations, 12 February 2013, in which steel mills with high levels of unutilized capacities were either shut down or reoriented towards innovations.

5   Producers and product mix

The sum and substance of the previous chapter has been the assertion that India has excess capacity, as well as excess production, which needs to be restricted (in order to firm up the prices of steel products in the domestic market). In order to pull back quantities in the market, the Ministry of Steel has imposed a Quality Control Order and set Minimum Import Prices of steel, by which the steel processors are forced to buy the more expensive steel from domestic producers. Since many of the units in the secondary steel sector process mill products like cold rolled sheets and electrical sheets, tin plates and pipes, from inputs like hot rolled and cold rolled sheets or hot rolled skelp; these smaller but specialized units close down as well. This means that, in a bid to protect the integrated steelmakers, we are harming the cause of the higher value added manufacturing and shrinking the base of manufacturing in India. We also appear to be on the anvil of a war between the large producers and the secondary sector, each having equal weightage in terms of tonnage of steel produced.[1] These conflicts are crucial in India, where the bulk of economic production rests on small producers, often very tiny enterprises owned by single owners.

The shaping of the steel industry of India: historical contingencies

Large plants and small rerollers

Before we proceed towards a more detailed analysis of the problem of overproduction and overcapacity, and the need to pare capacities and curtail production (so that prices remain steady in the market), we need to understand the structure of the Indian steel industry to understand how the present structure came to be. If we plot the developments in the Indian steel industry over time, then the picture emerges as follows. In the entire run between 1940 to the end of 1970s, the large integrated plants, comprising mainly of Tata Steel and SAIL plants, overwhelmingly produced semis to be rolled into bars and rods, and light structurals by the smaller rerollers, while they produced the wider flat sections, like HR coils, and even cold rolled coils. Flat steels are wider, and hence need larger equipment, which makes it difficult for the smaller producers to set up such facilities. The steel scenario therefore, was one of synergy, with the secondary rerollers rolling out the semis of integrated steel into bars and rods. Sometimes, of course, they would use the defective hot rolled steel sheets and then roll them out into cold rolled sheets. In fact, the first units of the cold rolled sheets in India were set up through the rolling of defectives from the large integrated plants and defectives that were non-usable for more sophisticated applications (but were thought to be perfect as sheets for use in rural areas and for other low-end uses such as drums, barrels, covering sheets and even air coolers and shades). Galvanizing facilities were set up, also, in the secondary sectors to zinc coat the cold rolled sheets: for making roof sheds, trunks and boxes, grain storage silos, cow pens and others items of rude and rudimentary character. There was little need for quality in steel, which was for sundry use by the individual. A slew of casting units produced high-value steel castings for machinery parts and other castings, such as manhole covers, both of which were major earners of export revenues. This was the picture we had in the middle of the 1970s.

Slight deregulation and the coming of the electric arc furnaces

It was by the end of the 1970s, and in the beginning of the 1980s, when the steel market expanded substantially, from less than 8 million tonnes in 1979, to over 10 million tonnes per annum, in 1983. Integrated steel plants needed large invest-ments, which were not always forthcoming in the Indian economy, and consumer demand went on increasing (in view of what would be the beginnings of an urban revolution in India). It was then that the rerollers, who were in the front line of steel use supplying bars and rods for domestic construction, wanted more supplies of semis (in order to be able to roll out more and more steel sections). For the first time, licenses were awarded to investors to set up electric arc furnaces, which used steel scrap for the manufacture of crude steel, in order to fill in the deficiency in semis.

All through the years after Independence, the Indian steel industry was con-trolled by means of industrial licenses. The entire philosophy of Independent India was to be able to meet domestic demand through indigenous industries. Hence, it was important that the domestic capacities for providing steel had to be set up, in order to meet, what seemed to be, an ever-rising demand. In order to supplement the supplies of semis from the integrated steel plants, licenses were awarded to interested investors in the electric arc furnaces, which produced smaller sized billets known as pencil ingots. In the 1980s and till the middle of the 1990s, the electric arc furnaces constituted an important (and valued sector of the society) to mitigate the deficiency in the supply of steel.

A major difference—between the electric arc furnaces of the western world and of India—is that the Indian furnaces produced largely mild steel, while those in the West were used for the production of high carbon steel and even silicon steel, specialized varieties for engineering uses (which neither had a mass market, nor needed to be produced on a mass scale). In the middle of the 1990s, yet another class of steel makers emerged on the Indian scenario, namely, the induction furnaces. The induction furnaces were essentially used in precious metals (such as gold, silver and copper), and were modified for the melting of stainless steel scrap. But, the Indian steelmakers used the contraption for melting mild steel scrap and producing ingots for the rerollers. The difference between the electric arc furnace and the induction furnace was that the latter had even lower capital costs than the former. The low capital costs lowered the barrier of entry into the business of steel, and soon, every kind of person connected with the steel business rushed to melt scrap and produce pencil ingots. These new "entrants" were raw material traders, mine owners, scrap collectors, transporters and so on, all of whom decided to take advantage of the new and cheap technology of induction melting to make steel, and then roll them for the market. Prices rose strongly throughout the 1990s, to peak in 1995, and there again, despite a slight hiccup in the Asian meltdown in 1997, rose fairly strongly on Chinese demand, up through the Beijing Olympics in 2008.

Integration at smaller scales through the induction furnace and the sponge iron plants: the great Indian innovation

Sometime, around the end of the 1990s, came the great Indian discovery of sponge iron, a form of directly reduced iron that changed the face of the Indian steel industry, lifting it up from the eighth largest steel producer to be among the top three, at present. Sponge iron is directly reduced iron in its solid form by the use of either natural gas or non-coking coal. Since India has a surfeit of non-coking coal, it used this as fuel and reductant to obtain sponge iron. Sponge iron was produced out of ore sized between 10 mm and 20 mm, a size that was mined from the deposits, when extracting lump ore of sizes above 20 mm. The lump ore fetched some sort of a market price, but fines, as the sizes between 10 to 20 mm were called, barely had any kind of price discovery. Sponge iron could add value to this and fetch prices as high as melting scrap. Two major technological innovations braced the induction furnace: one was the ability to use sponge iron, wholly, as raw material, and the other was to be able to refine the crude steel by an external attachment of ladle refining. The problem of degassing (that so irked steel made by melting scrap) was nearly eliminated in the induction furnaces; operating costs were lower, as well.[2] Induction furnaces produced cleaner steel, and since they used sponge iron, they could take advantage of the fact that the Indian iron ore was of superior quality. In effect, induction furnaces, with the use of sponge iron, were actually integrated and primary steel producers, albeit in small scale.

Induction furnaces and sponge iron together emerged as a distinct and definitive genre of steelmaking, and added substantially to the steelmaking capacity of the country. As long as the demand was buoyant, things seemed fine, but were demand to drop even slightly, then the extant supply of steel in the market was irksome. It was so cheap and easy to access the induction furnaces that it made it easy for steel to emerge out of the high cost economy into a nearly informal sector or cottage industry. Today, in the face of the collapsing demand and the need for the large sector to expand, this small segment of induction furnaces, which accounts for over 50% of the steelmaking capacity of India (and in itself is as large as the steel industry of France, Spain, Ukraine or Italy), stands to be cut to size.

We discussed in the preceding chapter that much of the steelmaking capacity is being set up because of arm-twisting of downstream producers by the large producers (from whom the former would conventionally source the intermediate products from the integrated plants). The galloping rise in steelmaking capacities by electric furnaces is largely, because the downstream processors now are organizing their own feed material in the form of semis.

Product mix of large and small plants

Table 5.1 shows the product mix of large integrated steel and secondary producers. The secondary sector produces bars and rods, structurals, CR coils, GP, GC sheets, tinplates and pipes, while the integrated oxygen-based plants produce HR coils and skelp, HR sheets and some CR coils, and in all probability auto-grade sheets, as well. The secondary sector is better poised to manufacture electrical steel sheets, and in fact, electrical sheets are produced in the electric arc furnaces in Austria, Luxembourg and the Netherlands and even Germany. As we can note from Table 5.2, bars and rods and GP/GC sheets are in excess supply, both of which are the preserve of the secondary sector. The product mix accrues due to the historical

Table 5.1 Production of steel items for the large and small producers in India in 2014–15

Items	Large integrated sector	Secondary small sector	Total steel produced
	In thousand tonnes		
Semis	23648	42898	66546
Bars and rods	9688	22733	32421
Structurals	1482	6025	7507
Railway material	830	5	835
Total non–flats	12000	28763	40763
Plates	4662	52	4714
HR coils/skelp	20029	5322	25351
HR sheets	1099	39	1138
CR coils/sheets	5271	5285	10556
GP/GC sheets	2998	4005	7003
Electrical sheets	69	71	140
Tin plates	0	354	354
Pipes	238	1856	2094
Total flats	34366	16984	51350
Total finished steel	46366	45747	92113

Source: JPC, 2016.

relations between the large and the small plants, and the fact that the small plants serve smaller and more localized markets for steel. The smaller plants now have certain levels of integration through the sponge iron and induction furnace routes, through which they produce mainly bars and rods; some larger electric arc furnaces produce HR coils, though not quite the wide sheets, but an overwhelming number of the players in the small segment are stand alone facilities (producing cold rolled sheets, galvanized sheets and in some cases even silicon steel sheets). The large plants are mainly producers of mild steel, wider and heavier sections that are made in bulk for the large customers, like the railways, oil and gas sector, large construction and so on. The product mix of the Indian steel industry reflects its market structure (in which a few large consumer sectors are supplemented by a large number of smaller consumers).

Product mix of excess supply

Table 5.2 suggests bars and rods and structurals are overproduced and so are the galvanized sheets. Interestingly, both are overwhelmingly produced in the secondary sector, and hence, there is a crying demand from the large producer lobbies that these smaller players be curtailed, as overproduction tends to reduce the market prices. The existing large steel producers do not wholly address the market demand for heavy sections, which only the large plants can make. Plates, HR coils and CR coils are in short supply, and these could well increase in supply.

Table 5.2 Production, consumption and excess supply of steel mill products in India in 2014–15

Products	Production for sale	Consumption	Excess supply
	In thousand tonnes		
Semis	43642	43451	191
Bars and rods	32251	31081	1170
Structurals	7495	7301	194
Railway materials	835	851	−16
Non-flats	40581	39233	1348
Plates	4700	4770	−70
HR coils/strip	20205	20543	−338
HR sheets	1138	1113	25
CR coils	7509	8526	−1017
GP/GC sheets	6892	5554	1338
Total flats	43031	31003	12028

Source: JPC, 2016 and own calculations.

In Table 5.3, the products which have been in short supply in terms of production are now observed to be in glut because of too many imports. No wonder then, that the large integrated steel producers cry because they want the imports to be stalled, so that they can produce to their capacities.

A reason why the products which are in short supply in the domestic industry are overimported is possibly because the landed costs, which include duties and taxes, work out to be cheaper than the domestic prices. Domestic products are more expensive when the plants produce at less than full capacity, and make such products vulnerable to imports.

From Table 5.4, it is clear that bars and rods, plates and GP sheets are naturally protected against imports, as the domestic prices are lower than the landed costs. Incidentally, these are also overproduced at home. It is possible that these products are inherently competitive and exports may well be considered for these products in a more systematic manner.

Plates are better off, in terms of inherent competitiveness, and the large integrated plants could produce these, rather than the hot rolled coils in which competence

Table 5.3 Production, consumption, imports and exports of steel products in India 2014–15

Products	Production for sale	Consumption	Excess supply	Exports	Excess supply mitigated through exports or net surplus supply	Imports	Glut due to imports
			In thousand tonnes				
Semis	43642	43451	191	640	-449	696	247
Bars and rods	32251	31081	1170	392	778	854	1632
Structurals	7495	7301	194	83	111	53	164
Railway materials	835	851	−16	3	−19	15	−4
Non flats	40581	39233	1348	478	870	922	1792
Plates	4700	4770	−70	559	−629	732	103
HR coils/ strip	20205	20543	−338	1320	−1658	2006	348
HR sheets	1138	1113	25	55	−30	79	49
CR coils	7509	8526	−1017	585	−1602	1713	111
GP/GC sheets	6892	5554	1338	1629	−291	444	153
Total flats	43031	31003	12028	4428	7600	5831	13431

Source: JPC, 2016 and own calculations.

Table 5.4 Prices of steel mill items in December 2013 in Rs/tonne, Mumbai

Mild steel (prime)	Landed costs	Export prices	Domestic price
Billets, slabs	34072	32077	41960
Re-rollable scrap	29288	35138	35450
Bars and rods	54087	42073	47610
Plates	53553	43702	49470
HR sheets	34225	41448	48010
HR coils/strip	37021	33604	48670
CR coils	45560	46325	54175
GP/GC sheets/coils	59938	52922	56050

Source: JPC, 2016. Domestic prices reflect prices as of December 2013.

seems to be wanting. Therefore, the integrated plants may be encouraged to produce more plates. Plates are used mainly by cold rollers, especially for engineering applications; countries with developed engineering and machine building capabilities, especially the CIS countries, have very good uses for plates. In India, the new kinds of infrastructure, in terms of bridges, flyovers, ports and high-rise buildings, may see the use of steel plates and construction may become a major consumer of steel plates in the country.

Global competitiveness in terms of price

We used the value of the INR prevailing in the four quarters of 2015 and compared prices prevailing in India, EU, Asia, CIS and North America. As far as HR coils is concerned, the prices in India are higher than anywhere in the world, except in the USA, whose markets are heavily protected. In the case of CR coils, we observe a similar pattern, where the prices in India are the highest except in North America. Therefore, in the case of HR coils and CR coils, India does not appear to be too competitive. Yet, these are the products in which there exists a deficit in production in relation to demand; were India to expand production in these segments, albeit with the help of protection against imports, it would only move into a realm of uncompetitive steel production and waste natural resources in doing so. Since India is a country which exports iron ore and has one of the largest productions of sponge iron, an iron derivative, expansion into areas of less competitive steel production may reduce the overall resource efficiency of the country.

Let us now observe the case of bars and rods, as in Table 5.5. Bars and rods, which the secondary steel units produce, are inherently competitive, while the HR coils and CR coils in which the large integrated plants dominate, are inherently noncompetitive. The excess supply of bars and rods is therefore, an opportunity to push exports of these products.

Table 5.5 Global prices vs. Indian prices of steel mill products

In INR	Euro	USD	EU	Asia	North America	CIS	India
Exchange rate			*Hot rolled coils in Rs/tonne*				
Jan-15	73.7	62.3	30807	30153	40993	25481	33000
Jul-15	71.45	64.25	28223	26278	34824	28848	27950
Sep-15	76.1	67.05	28538	25412	34397	25010	27145
Dec-15	71.65	67.25	22856	23067	29926	22865	25800
Exchange rate			*Cold rolled coils in Rs/tonne*				
In INR	*Euro*	*USD*	*EU*	*Asia*	*North America*	*CIS*	*India*
Jan-15	73.7	62.3	36113	35075	46476	28907	38100
Jul-15	71.45	64.25	34296	30647	40799	24479	32210
Sep-15	76.1	67.05	35387	30575	40833	29703	32200
Dec-15	71.65	67.25	29735	28447	35306	28312	30430
Exchange rate			*Merchant bars in Rs/tonne*				
In INR	*Euro*	*USD*	*EU*	*Asia*	*North America*	*CIS*	*India*
Jan-15	73.7	62.3	37071	34016	52519	29468	31000
Jul-15	71.45	64.25	36511	31932	47031	29041	26400
Sep-15	76.1	67.05	38126	30977	47404	26954	26200
Dec-15	71.65	67.25	33389	28918	43645	23201	22400

Source: www.steelonthenet.com; exchange rate (published by the Ministry of Finance, India).

Price ladder across the value chain: paradox of import protection

We now track the price differential along the value chain, which means that we observe the difference in prices between the previous stages of production to a later stage of production. For instance, we take the difference in prices between TMT bars and billets, the difference between CR coils and HR coils and so on. Table 5.6 presents two kinds of scenarios; one in which both the input material and the output are locally procured and produced, and the other where the input is imported and output sold locally.

Table 5.6 reflects that for almost every mill product in India, imported inputs, rather than domestically produced inputs, would improve price margins. A possible explanation for this is that stand-alone plants with reheating do much better than integrated plants with an unbroken chain of processing. Since India is

Table 5.6 Price differences in progressive processing of steel mill products in Mumbai

Price differentials in Rs/tonne	Domestic price differences as of December 2015	Input is imported and sales are in the domestic market
Billet to bar	5650.00	13537.81
Rerollable scrap to bar	14020.00	18322.40
Slabs to HR sheets	400.00	13937.81
HR coils to CR coils	−800.00	17153.89
HR coils to GP/GC sheets	6165.00	19028.89
CR coils to GP/GC sheets	7380.00	10489.99

Source: Calculated from JPC Prices in Annual Statistics 2014-15.

Table 5.7 Global and Indian price differences along the value chain in steel mill products

Items	Global prices in USD per tonne	Value addition in USD per tonne over the previous item in global prices	JPC prices	Value addition in Rs per tonne in Indian domestic market prices	Value addition in India in USD per tonne
Iron ore	60		5500		
Pig iron	320	260	23000	17500	260
Slab	376	56	31600	8600	128
HRC	441	65	32725	1125	17
CRC	574	133	35044	2319	34
Hot dip galvanizing	687	113	47520	12476	185
Coated sheets	814	127			

Source: www.steelonthenet.com and JPC Bulletins. JPC Prices are for H3 2015 and www.steelonthenet .com prices are for H1 2015.

more comfortable in batch production in stand-alone plants, and uncomfortable in integrated mills, it is better to have a lot of imported inputs for downstream processing in fragmentary mills. Protection against imports might retard the downstream industries and expand the opportunities for large integrated steel plants, for they would now absorb their input and produce final products along the value chain. Autarky and the production of downstream products by the large integrated plants would reduce the overall value of the steel industry and encouraging the smaller producers would actually increase it.

Presented in Table 5.7 is a comparative scenario of price differentials, as we proceed along the value chain of steel.

Table 5.7 is once again, an iteration of all that has gone before; namely, were India to concentrate on the production of pig iron, slabs and hot dip galvanizing, rather than pursuing the health of HR and CR production, the overall value of the steel industry would improve.

Conclusions about products and product mix

We may conclude that the production of the secondary mills, namely of bars and rods and galvanized flats, is inherently more price competitive, and hence is naturally protected against imports. These products have also proliferated in the Indian markets so that we now have an excess supply of these products; it might do us well to pursue an active policy of exports for these products.

The hot rolled coils and cold rolled coils, mostly produced by the large integrated producers, are weaker where price competition is concerned; they are unable to withstand the pressure of global prices, and these are the products in which production remains deficient, with respect to supply.

India does far better by importing intermediate mill products for downward processing in stand-alone and fragmentary mills rather than in integrated mills; it might be a better idea to encourage the smaller processors than to insist on integrated facilities with continuous casting and rolling.

While there is little need to discourage imports, there is a strong need to encourage exports in a systematic way.

Notes

1   The share of the integrated steel mills through the oxygen route is 51% of the total finished steel produced in 2014-15. JPC, 2016.
2   www.dsir.gov.in/reports/techreps/tsr154.pdf

6 Who to promote, the integrated mills or electric furnaces?

It is clear that with the overcapacity and the oversupply of steel both in India as well as across the world, that one has to think of curtailing capacities for some of the steel mills. In order to identify the relatively more inefficient capacities, we often resort to capacity utilization rates; those plants with lower rates of capacity utilization may be identified for closures by banks, or by the government bodies or industry bodies. We observe the capacity utilization rates of the Indian steel segments in Table 6.1. Sponge iron and electric arc furnaces have done poorly, while the oxygen-based plants and the induction furnaces have done better and pig iron production could do with more addition in capacity.

Shift from integrated oxygen plants to smaller electric steelmaking facilities in order to deal with excess capacity

It is very interesting to note, that both in the USA and for many countries, like Belgium, Italy, Finland and others in the EU, the strategy to deal with global overcapacity has been to replace the oxygen furnaces with smaller electric furnaces.[1] Laplace Conseil observes that the world is globalized and huge excess capacities across the world, especially driven by China, are creating a serious glut in the steel market, that the demand for steel in developed countries is stagnant, that the margins from the production of steel are falling and that such overcapacity is persistent and is here to stay. Under these circumstances, it is only to be expected that capacities will be cut, but the consultants insist that the way forward in the situation of glut is to replace oxygen furnaces by electric furnaces.[2] But, India appears to be doing just the opposite, displacing the electric steelmaking facilities, namely the induction furnaces, with integrated steel plants. The share of electric furnaces and the induction furnaces together in India consist of 48% of the steelmaking capacity. The share of electric steel in the EU is around 42%, while that in the USA is 62% and EU has a larger scrap "mine" than the USA. The idea behind the preference for electric furnaces is to be able to use "local" raw material, namely scrap and support local needs; they are easy to shut down and start up and hence, demand and supply are better balanced. The strategy that Laplace Conseil suggests for the steel industry in order to adapt to a persistent supply glut is to shift from oxygen furnaces into electric steelmaking.[3]

Table 6.1 Structure of the Indian steel industry 2013-14

Segment	Number of working units	Capacity in million tonnes	Number of closed units	Capacity in million tonnes	Production in million tonnes	Capacity utilization in %
Integrated oxygen–based plants	13	35.55			35.52	100
Electric arc furnace	47	25.76			18.59	72
Induction furnace	1321	33.95			27.58	81
Pig iron	19	4.83			7.95	165
Sponge iron	324	37.3			22.87	61
HR wide sheets	1760	30.98	568	4.21		
HR narrow strips	12	14.39				
CR sheets/ strips	65	9.55				
Steel wire drawing	35	0.71	65	0.73		
GP/GC sheets	20	5.06				
Tin plates	1	0.10	2	0.11		

Source: Ministry of Steel, Annual Report, 2015.

It is wise to keep steel capacities small and fragmented because then, one does not have to keep holding on to the large indivisible capacities, piling up bad debts during economic downturns and demand depressions. Small capacities are flexible, and no wonder then, that Laplace Conseil suggests these as the way forward in times of market and demand volatility of steel.

Costs of making steel through electric furnaces are lower

Laplace Conseil calculates the costs of setting up of an integrated plant at USD 800 to 1200 per tonne of steel produced, while the costs of setting up an electric arc furnace are only USD 150 to 300 per tonne of finished steel. India uses induction furnaces, whose CAPEX costs are even lower. Annual maintenance costs are 7% of the CAPEX for both processes, and while the oxygen furnaces may need coke oven batteries costing anywhere between 300 and 400 million USD,[4] the induction furnaces in India may need sponge iron and sometimes pellet plants, which might raise the costs of setting up an "integrated" steelmaking capacity in the electric furnace sector to about USD 350 per tonne. In terms of the CAPEX, the induction furnace definitely does better.

The electric arc furnaces, known in India as mini steel plants, further dissolved into the induction furnaces. The problem with the electric arc furnace was that nearly 70% of its costs consisted of electricity, and with electricity being costly in India, and the energy economy of the electric furnaces not effective below a 40 tonne furnace capacity, it made sense for the entrepreneurs to seek the even smaller induction furnaces for lower CAPEX costs and a better operating economy.[5] Smaller producers, with modest financial powers, could now produce steel as well as the multi-millionaire entrepreneurs of the integrated steel plants. The technology of the induction furnace made it possible for the base of the Indian steel industry to expand substantially.

Tables 6.2a and 6.2b reveal what is commonsensically known to the Indian policy makers, which is that the integrated steel plants have lower operational costs than the electric furnaces. But, Tables 6.2a and 6.2b hold true only when the debts on CAPEX

Table 6.2a Basic oxygen furnace route steelmaking costs 2016: conversion costs for BOF steelmaking

Item in USD/unit	Factor	Unit	Unit cost	Fixed	Variable	Total
Iron ore	1.559	tonne	51.63	0	80.49	80.49
Iron ore transport	1.559	tonne	5.8	0	9.04	9.04
Coal	0.892	tonne	82.12	0	73.25	73.25
Coal transport	0.892	tonne	4.22	0	3.77	3.77
Steel scrap	0.15	tonne	160.65	0	24.1	24.1
Steel scrap transport	0.15	tonne	5	0	0.75	0.75
Industrial gases	262	cu metres	0.07	0	18.05	18.05
Ferro alloys	0.006	tonne	1383	0	7.7	7.7
Fluxes	0.536	tonne	37.5	0	20.1	20.1
Refractories	0.011	tonne	685	0	7.71	7.71
Other costs	1	unit	15.48	3.87	11.61	15.48
Byproduct credits	1	unit	−4.44	0	−4.44	−4.44
Thermal energy net	−7.769	GJ	4.35	0	−33.8	−33.8
Electricty	0.141	MWh	127	2.69	15.22	17.91
Labour	0.518	hours	30.56	3.96	11.87	15.83
Capital charges	1	unit	53.63	53.63	0	53.63
Total				64.15	245.42	309.57

Source: www.steelonthenet.com

Table 6.2b Electric arc furnace steelmaking costs 2016: conversion costs for electric arc steelmaking

Item in USD/unit	Factor	Unit	Unit cost	Fixed	Variable	Total
Steel scrap	1.113	tonne	160.65	0	178.75	178.75
Steel scrap transport	1.113	tonne	5	0	5.56	5.56
Pig iron/DRI	0	tonne	174.99	0	0	0
Pig iron/DRI transport	0	tonne	14	0	0	0
Industrial gases	17	cu metres	0.07	0	1.2	1.2
Ferro alloys	0.009	tonne	1383	0	12.61	12.61
Fluxes	0.031	tonne	118	0	3.67	3.67
Electrodes	0.005	tonne	5790	0	29.41	29.41
Refractories	0.009	tonne	685	0	6.24	6.24
Other costs	1	tonne	10.2	2.55	7.65	10.2
Thermal energy	-0.396	GJ	4.35	0	−1.72	−1.72
Electricity	0.455	MWh	127	8.66	49.08	57.74
Labour	0.349	hours	30.56	2.67	8.01	10.68
Capital charges	1	unit	17.77	17.77	0	17.77
Total				31.65	300.46	332.11

Source: www.steelonthenet.com

loans have been cleared by both kinds of steel plants. The costs of setting up Greenfield integrated plants in the oxygen route are much larger than those in the electric furnaces, and the burden of debt on the former is larger. For settled economies, the operating costs of integrated plants are lower than those of the electric furnaces, but in times of expansion, the integrated plants put a lot of pressure on banks and other lending bodies for loans. We may suggest that in times as the present, when the Ministry of Steel has set a target of expanding steel capacities to 300 million tonnes, steel capacities can be added more economically in the induction furnace sector because some capacities here can be closed down more easily, in case of excess capacity spikes in the short term.

Social and environmental costs of large steel plants

Steel is one of the most polluting industries in the world. This is why one should be careful to reckon the carbon dioxide emissions, as well, from the various processes of making steel. Clearly here the integrated steel plants are the largest producers of carbon dioxide, while the EAF with cold DRI or with scrap do the best. By

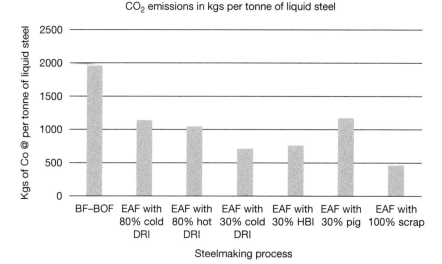

CO$_2$ emissions in kgs per tonne of liquid steel

Figure 6.1 CO$_2$ emissions in the various steelmaking processes

Source: Prakash Tatia. *Green Steel Making – Gas Based Technology for Sponge Iron Industry* (Welspun Maxsteel Ltd), 2014.

substituting EAF with induction furnaces, our parameters can only improve.[6] There appears to be a drop of over 60% in terms of carbon emission.

Drawbacks of induction furnaces

Too much dependence on the quality of raw materials

One drawback of the induction furnace is that despite the fact that it is the cleanest way of producing steel with almost no emissions, its capabilities for refining steel are limited. Therefore, induction furnaces have to depend on the quality of raw material for the quality of the output. Nowhere in the world, except in India, have induction furnaces been used to produce mild steel to the extent of nearly 28 million tonnes per annum, higher than the production of countries like France, Spain, Poland and only slightly lower than countries like Brazil and the Ukraine. The induction furnace is dependent upon the quality of raw material for its sustenance as a quality producer of steel. The dependence on the quality of raw materials made induction furnaces depend on sponge iron, where the metallic quality can be controlled by choosing the right kind of iron ore. Indeed, some induction furnaces in India have grown to nearly 30 tonne furnaces in size and produce good quality low carbon steel.

In recent times since 2008, when China started buying iron ore at mind-blowing high prices and was importing almost without limits, there was a rush to extract as much iron ore as possible, on the one hand, and export the best quality to China, on the other. Excess mining, on the one hand, and using only leftovers for the domestic market, leaving the best quality for exports, seriously compromised the quality of iron ore, and thereafter, the quality of sponge iron. The industry body representing the induction furnaces has raised the issue of a Quality Control Order on sponge iron in order to ensure that the induction furnaces produce quality steel. The mineral policy pertaining to iron ore must take into account the quality of iron ore, says the association of induction furnaces.[7]

Integrated steel plants are supposed to do best with raw materials

Since India is proud of its iron ore resources, policy makers have a bias towards the integrated steel plants based on blast furnaces. We must also remember that India started its steel production with blast furnaces during its struggle for freedom and hence, the integrated oxygen route has flavours of nationalism. Policy makers also feel that it is the oxygen route in which raw materials constitute much lower proportions of the total costs, and margins for steel over raw material costs are supposed to be the widest. In Tables 6.2a and 6.2b, on costs we observe that price differentials between iron ore and coal and finished steel are much wider than the price differentials between steel scrap, or the DRI and finished steel.

Financial performance of steel companies

Presented in Table 6.3 are averages from the annual reports of FY(14–15) for the listed companies only. For the large integrated steel plants, yearly results for SAIL, Tata Steel and JSW have been considered. For the small and medium cap sized firms, we have considered Jindal Stainless Steel, Mukand Steel, Adhunik, Rathi, Usha Martin and Electrosteel Limited. For the rolling mills, Sujana Steels, Sunflag, Rathi Alloys, ISMT Metals and Kalyani Steels have been considered. For the HR/CR segment, Bhushan Steels, Pennar Steels, Steelco, Mahamaya and Ruchi Strips have been considered. Among the GP/GC sheet segment, we have considered Uttam Galva, Shree Precoated, Vardhaman and Jai Corp.

The results tell us the following:

- The investments/total assets indicate the growth in capacities and activities of the companies. The large integrated steel plants show the most robust growth in capacities, followed by the GP/GC segment.
- The inventory turnover ratio is the best for the rolling mills, which goes to show that bars and rods and light structurals are the fastest moving commodity in our steel industry, while the HR/CR tends to pile up stocks.
- Raw materials constitute the highest proportion of costs for the GP/GC sheets, showing that they are material processing units; the integrated plants have the lowest percentage of raw materials as a percentage of sales, showing that they have a substantial value addition. Raw material prices, which are HR sheets for the galvanizers, are crucial and hence, are likely to be most affected by trade protectionism, while the integrated steel mills have more capacity to absorb fluctuations in iron ore and coking coal prices, which are their raw materials. SAIL and Tata Steel have captive mines.

Table 6.3 Relative performances of various categories of steel companies in India

Results from 2014–15	Large integrated	Small and medium steel producers	Rolling mills	HR/CR	GP/GC
Net profit/net sales %	8.01	−4.2	−4.95	−9.82	1.32
PBDIT/net sales %	20.29	15.77	8.61	18.13	8.52
Inventory turnover ratio	3.89	2.92	5.84	1.63	5.72
Raw materials/net sales %	46.38	65.22	75.31	62.71	83.01
Power and fuels/net sales %	8.69	8.94	6.96	10.78	1.64
Labour costs/net sales %	11.46	3.68	3.43	2.54	2.1
Investments/total assets %	27.25	1.95	10.6	1.46	15.35

Source: www.MoneyControl.com

- Power costs are proportionally the highest in the HR/CR segment, while labour costs appear to be the highest proportion of net sales for the integrated plants, naturally because of the liberal wages and other allowances.
- Net profits are only slight for the GP/GC sheets and negative for other segments, except for the integrated steel plants; we may well say that the net profits are positive only for the large plants. The relatively better profits for the integrated steel plants are made possible by the lower proportion of raw material costs, attracting investments into this sector.

Value additions for different producer segments

We encounter yet another paradox when we look at the value additions along the processed products from the materials, which emanate from the integrated plants, and those which emanate from the induction furnaces. Table 6.4a presents the value additions that have been considered in terms of price differences. The exercise is notional because angles, joists and channels cannot be really drawn from scrap, though bars and rods can easily be done, but the calculations suggest that when one directly rolls scrap, it gives the best margins. No wonder that there exists a large base of scrap rerollers who roll out scrap directly, especially the ship-breaking scrap. Between billets and pencil ingots, margins improve with the use of pencil ingots, thus suggesting that the rolling mills which are attached to induction furnaces do far better than those who roll semis from integrated steel plants. The margins are best when scrap is directly rerolled into rounds and wire rods and even tor steel.

Table 6.4a Price differences for value-added products from scrap, billets and pencil ingots, December 2015, Mumbai

Products	Mumbai prices as of December 2015 in Rs/tonne	Value addition in Rs/tonne from…			
		HMS 1	Billets	Billets via blooms	Pencil ingots
Wire rods 6mm	32189	10189	589	−30311	4089
Wire rods 8 mm	32189	10189	589	−30311	4089
Rounds 10 mm	34683	12683	3083	−27817	6583
Rounds 16 mm	34683	12683	3083	−27817	6583
Rounds 25 mm	34683	12683	3083	−27817	6583
Tor TMT 10 mm	30633	8633	-967	−31867	2533
Tor TMT 12 mm	30340	8340	-1260	−32160	2240
Tor TMT 25 mm	30340	8340	-1260	−32160	2240
Angles 50 × 5 0 × 6 mm	32167	10167	567	−30333	4067
Angles 75 × 75 × 6 mm	32550	10550	950	−29950	4450
Joists 125 × 70 mm	40425	18425	8825	−22075	12325
Joists 200 × 100 mm	34125	12125	2525	−28375	6025
Channels 75 × 40 mm	33732	11732	2132	−28768	5632
Channels 150 × 75 mm	34073	12073	2473	−28427	5973

Source: Constructed from JPC Bulletin, January 2016.

If we are to proceed in the conventional route from ingots to blooms to billets, then our margins would turn negative and such a process would be unsustainable; yet, the picture looks bright with the use of pencil ingots. The billet via bloom appears to be the historical path when rolling mills would roll out bars and rods and sections from blooms and billets from the integrated mills. The above exercise shows that such conventional mills are now uneconomical. However, rolling mills which use pencil ingots from the induction furnaces, are doing well, and their bonding with the latter on the one hand, and the sponge iron and induction furnace bond on the other, make for a nice integrated circuit of steel production of iron, steel and mill products. In terms of higher price differentials, such circuits of stand-alone facilities do well.

We turn to the flat steels in Table 6.4b.

Interestingly, when we consider price differences from slabs to plates and to HR coils, CR Coils and others, margins improve in the integrated processes because slabs are produced by the integrated plants. Overall, price gains could result, were the flats entirely produced by the integrated plants. Despite such advantages the integrated plants do not produce enough HR sheets because there is unmet demand in this segment, as we observed in the previous chapter. Unfortunately, for India, the prices of flats are high only because of protection against imports; were imports to take place freely in India, it is possible that the stand-alone cold rollers and galvanizers would have done very well.

Table 6.4b Price differences for value-added products from slabs, HR coils and CR coils, December 2015, Mumbai

	JPC prices in Mumbai, December 2015	Price addition in Rs/tonne for various categories from slabs	
Plates 6 mm	32725	1825	
Plates 10 mm	32419	1519	
Plates 12 mm	32419	1519	
Plates 25 mm	32463	1563	
HR coils 2 mm	32725	1825	
HR coils 2.5 mm	32463	1563	
HR coils 3.15 mm	32288	1388	
		From HR coils	*From slabs*
CR coils 0.63 mm	35044	2319	4144
CR coils 1 mm	35088	2363	
		From CR coils	
GP sheets 0.4mm	47520	12476	16620
GP sheets 0.63 mm	46594	11506	
GC heets 0.4 mm	47119	12075	
GC sheets 0.63 mm	45675	10631	

Source: Constructed from JPC Bulletin, January 2016.

Conclusions

We have confusing images when we consider the integrated sector and the small and fragmentary small steelmakers, in terms of their various parameters. The integrated producers do better than the smaller players, in terms of capacity utilization, which means that they have more economical operations than the smaller players. However, the smaller furnaces are more flexible and they can adapt easily to needs of capacity reduction, or may bring into operations more capacity in times of market upswings. Costs of operation of electric furnaces are higher than those of the integrated plants, only when the CAPEX costs are covered; the CAPEX costs of integrated steel plants are at least five times as much as the electric furnaces and eight times as high as that of an induction furnace. In terms of pollution, electric furnaces have lower emissions than the integrated plants. Profit margins are much lower in the secondary steel mills, but price differences between the input material and the finished products are higher than for the integrated mills. Prices, which prevail in the domestic markets, are adequate for the secondary sector, but not for the integrated plants, who seem to need trade protection all the time. Costs of raw materials are lower for the integrated sector. With these outcomes, which kind of steel facility should we promote?

We are operating in abnormal times of excess steel capacities, where the Indian steel industry faces overcapacity. We are also operating in times in which the scope for protection against imports has a limited timespan and eventually one has to allow free trade to set in. The integrated mills are not comfortable producing hot rolled coils in the most economical way, and yet, due to their advantages in raw materials they make the best profits. Expansion of the integrated sector is thus, lucrative for the stock exchanges, but may be uncomfortable for the overall competitiveness of the economy. The smaller producers have less profitability and they are willing to work on much lower earnings, but they guarantee consumers of steel mill products prices that are globally competitive and may be said to satisfy consumer needs far better than large corporations. The large mills are high CAPEX mills, which may do very well in an ascending industry, but steel, as it is produced in the world today, has become a sunset industry in which capacity additions, through small fractional plants, may be better for the economy of steel-producing countries on the whole.

Notes

1   *EAF vs BOF. Strategies for Overcapacity*. Laplace Conseil. 2012. www.oecd.org/sti/ind/Item%209.%20Laplace%20-%20Steel%20Energy.pdf and OECD (2015), "Excess Capacity in the Global Steel Industry and the Implications of New Investment Projects", *OECD Science, Technology and Industry Policy Papers*, No. 18, OECD Publishing. http://dx.doi.org/10.1787/5js65x46nxhj-en OECD.
2   Ibid.
3   Ibid.
4   Ibid.
5   Comprehensive Industry Document on Electric Arc Furnaces and Induction Furnaces. CPCB. March 2010, p. 11.
6   Comprehensive Industry Document on EAFs and Induction Furnaces. CPCB. Delhi. 2010, p. 46.
7   Kamal Agarwal, Secretary General, All India Induction Furnace, Delhi, various forums.

7 The failure of demand of steel in India

This chapter tries to address the problem of demand failure in the Indian steel industry. Demand failure in the Indian steel industry has manifested in the form of consumption of finished steel being persistently lower than that of its production, leading to a situation of excess production, price depression and the wiping off of margins in the steel industry; this has left many a firm debt strapped.

According to a report written by Deepak Sahu in Infracircle,[1] the Indian steel industry is in deep distress, having accumulated a debt of Rs 3.1 trillion. Assuming that a million tonnes of fresh capacity of steelmaking needs Rs 7000 crores to be set up, the debts with the industry could easily add 43 million tonnes of capacity in the country. Assuming that a tonne of steel from the integrated plants sell at Rs 60,000 a tonne, this amount of debt means that there should be a circulation of at least 50 million tonnes more for the industry to tide over this debt. This, to my mind, is the deficiency of demand. Such levels of demand will raise the per capita steel consumption close to 100 kgs. The failure of demand is notional because much higher levels of demand for steel were projected, perhaps to "park" gigantic funds of promoters in the form of steel projects.

The present chapter addresses the possible reasons for the failure of demand for steel, namely the infrastructure projects that did not take off, the slowing down of the steel-consuming sectors and the overestimation of demand (because the tools were not realistic). The chapter also discusses the extent of overproduction (in terms of the product mix of the country). Historically, India has always been a country with supply constraints, when more and more steel capacity needed to be added to satisfy an ever-growing demand; it is only after the economic liberalization that the steel supply came to be in surplus.

Projected demand versus production and consumption

Table 7.1 gives a picture of the anticipated demand that far outstrips production, and production that outstrips consumption; clearly, the imagination of the steel industry is more optimistic than there is reason to be. Policy makers have exaggerated the demand for steel; and perhaps the demand projections are responsible for misleading the steel producers into imagining that there is more demand than what is on the ground.

Table 7.1 Excess supply in the market of total finished steel, alloy and non-alloy in India

Years	Projected demand	Consumption	Production for sale
	In thousand tonnes		
2011–12	72.6	71	75.7
2012–13	79.2	73.5	81.7
2013–14	86.4	74.1	87.7
2014–15	94.3	77	92.2

Source: Working Group for the Twelfth Five Year Plan, and JPC.

Table 7.2 Production and consumption of finished steel in India

	Production of steel	Consumption of steel	Projected demand
	In million tonnes		
2008–09	56.42	52.05	54.68
2009–10	59.69	52.35	59.47
2010–11	66.01	59.34	64.68
2011–12	73.42	70.92	70.34
2012–13	81.68	73.49	
2013–14	87.68	74.1	
2014–15	92.16	77	

Source: JPC, 2016.

Perhaps a reason for the policy makers' optimism lies in the faster growth of consumption, when compared to the growth of production before the economic liberalization, especially the 1980s, the decade of the economic high. JPC changed the parameters and many of the variables in the demand function, relooked at the revised projections of the GDP, and produced Table 7.2, with much lower projections for demand.

Pre-liberalization and post-liberalization phases of the steel industry in India

The decade before the economic liberalization, namely the 1980s, was a time of an economic high for India, and clearly the consumption and the production of steel jumped. Consumption forever remained above that of production. The pre-liberalization scope for expansion in steel gave reason for the overoptimism in steelmaking, and soon as many as 273 million tonnes worth of MoUs were signed in the states of Jharkhand, Odisha, Karnataka, Andhra Pradesh and West Bengal, all mineral-rich states. We may peruse the trends in steel production and consumption in Tables 7.3 and 7.4, provided below.

Indeed, in the years between 1983 and 1994, consumption always outstripped demand and imports filled in the gaps. Steel facilities were put up in the small sector to fill in the gaps in domestic demand, while capacities increased in the integrated steel plants in order to substitute imports with indigenous production. If we

Table 7.3 Trends in growth of production and consumption of steel in India

Period	Production in million tonnes	Consumption in million tonnes	CAGR of production in %	CAGR of consumption in %
Decade preceding deregulation 1982-83 to 1991-92	8.48 to 14.23	9.26 to 14.84	5.9	5.3
Decades after deregulation 1992-93 to 2010-11	16.89 to 66.01	15.81 to 65.61	8.4	8.1

Source: Report of the Working Group on Steel Industry for the Twelfth Five Year Plan (2012 to 2017)

Table 7.4 Historical trends in production and consumption of steel in India

Year	Production	Consumption
	In million tonnes	
1982-83	9.13	10.5
1983-84	8.5	9.86
1984-85	8.78	9.56
1985-86	10.03	10.76
1986-87	10.54	11.88
1987-88	11.95	12.81
1988-89	13.36	14.13
1989-90	13.4	14.12
1990-91	13.83	14.55
1991-92	14.63	14.86
1992-93	15.51	15.42
1993-94	15.2	14.92
1994-95	17.22	17.65

Source: JPC

consider Table 7.2 along with Table 7.3, we can easily see how post-2008, demand remained below that of production.

Cycles in the Indian steel industry: pre- and post-economic liberalization

We now turn to cycles in the Indian steel industry; steel being a cyclical industry, cycles are very common. The steel cycles before liberalization were small and short and the trend was always on the rise, with the peaks of present period higher than the peak of previous periods and so on. But, the cycles post 2008-09 show in U-turn, with the growth in steel having peaked in 2010, but thereafter falling steadily (Figures 7.1a and 7.1b).

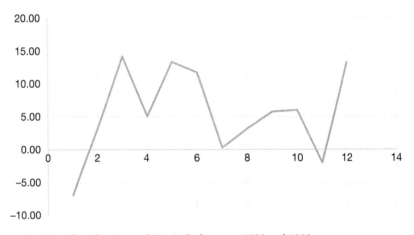

Figure 7.1a Steel production cycles in India between 1983 and 1993

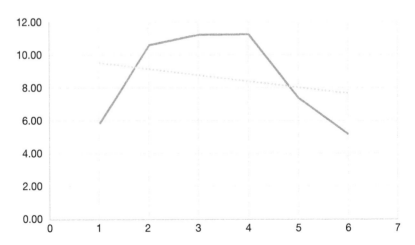

Figure 7.1b Steel production cycles in India between 2008 and 2014

While the phenomenon of excess production may be temporary, in general, there is a downward trend of steel consumption. When we compare the downward trend of Figure 7.1b with the upward trend of the Figure 7.1a, we get the uncomfortable feeling that steel production in India has already peaked, much like the advanced countries getting satiated or entering a low level of equilibrium. The Indian policy makers often deny that there is anything called excess supply of steel and insist that the investments in infrastructure will soon absorb all the additional steel that India may produce. A small exercise below will bust the belief.

Why has demand failed in India? Some possible answers

The time has now come to understand why demand has failed in India. In a growing economy as India, demand for steel should rise, especially as its economy is buoyant and growth is promising. Yet, we have a situation in steel, which is not unlike that in the advanced countries, where demand appears to have been satiated. Does this point to a low level of equilibrium in the steel industry?

Not demand failure but excess supply globally

It may be possible that demand has not failed, but instead production of steel has outstripped the demand growth for steel in the country (see Table 7.5).

Table 7.5 Excess production of crude steel across global regions

Region	In 2004	In 2013
	In thousand tonnes	
European Union	13258	12922
Other Europe	−680	−1183
CIS	68458	41201
North America	−38527	−30072
South America	11405	−5734
Africa	−3114	−20705
Middle East	−18067	−28098
Asia	−32072	34778
Oceania	−515	−1932
World	145	1177

Source: Steel Statistical Yearbook, 2014 and own calculations.

The failure of the private sector to bring in demand for steel

The major difference between the period before 1993 and the one after lies in the fact that India remained a regulated economy till about 1991. This means that the onus of public investments, most of which drive the demand for steel, now lies with the private sector rather than with the public sector. The Economic Survey 2014-15 clearly observes that the shift of onus to the private sector is the sole cause of the economic downturn.[2] Though banks collected money through the Jan Dhan Scheme and channelized these into the private sector, the initiatives of the private players and their implementation capabilities were much lower than expected. A part of the reason is perhaps the total lack of capability in project implementation, especially in executing large infrastructure projects. The money was taken from the bank and then not spent, or spent wastefully.[3]

Increase in steel consumption is incremental while the increase in production capacities are bulky

The trend of growth of consumption of steel has been slower than that of the growth of production. A possible reason for this could be that the consumption grows incrementally in small quantities, but production must grow in bulk (due to the indivisible nature of steelmaking capacities). However, in the decade before liberalization, the consumption of steel was higher than the production of steel. This trend is reversed with liberalization, when consumption lies consistently below production. A possible reason for this could be that post-liberalization, capacities were added enthusiastically in the integrated sector, while before liberalization, the growth in capacities was being led by the smaller, secondary steel producers, which added smaller capacities, and were better balanced against consumption.

Investments into infrastructure is slowing down demand

The Working Group Report on the Indian steel industry for the Twelfth Five Year Plan clearly mentions that infrastructure is expected to be the cornerstone of the growth of demand for steel in India.[4] The investments into infrastructure for the entire Twelfth Five Year Plan period was Rs 40,99,240 crores. If 15% of this is the spending on steel, that is Rs 6,14,886 crores. If the average value of steel during this period was Rs 40,000, then the entire period of the 12th FYP would absorb 153 million tonnes of steel, or about 30 million tonnes of steel. Unfortunately, this has not been the case, and truly, exactly 30 million tonnes of steelmaking capacity appear to be surplus in the steel industry.

In the announcement of the Union Budget, 2016, the outlay on infrastructure projects is Rs 2.21 lakh crore.[5] Assuming that 15% of this project outlay will be the spending on steel, one can calculate that the spending on steel will be Rs 0.33 lakh crores. Assuming that the steel used will be priced at Rs 60,000 on average, the quantities of steel used annually (due to the new projects in infrastructure) will be 5.52 million tonnes. We have also calculated that the excess supply of steel in India is to the tune of 15 million tonnes, in an earlier chapter. It is clear that the extra demand due to infrastructure projects will clear only a third of the excess supplies. We have also observed that net imports are to the tune of merely 3 million tonnes, which means that they have a marginal role in the supply glut of steel in India.

The slowdown in the steel-consuming sectors

From Table 7.6, we observe that the conventional steel-consuming sectors (like automobiles, engineering, construction and metal products) have slowed down substantially, while sectors like power generation and infrastructure have gained ground; these sectors, by themselves, cannot absorb all the steel manufactured in the country.

Was the forecast demand too high?

It is entirely possible that there is nothing wrong with the demand for steel in India, and that the forecasters have exaggerated the demand for steel (in order to make the sector look attractive to bankers and investors). The projected demand in each of the following years have been more than the consumption, but producers have invested ahead of the demand projections. We may refer to Table 7.2, right at the beginning of the chapter, to observe that demand was projected too optimistically than what was the case, and in fact, JPC reduced the projections towards reality, subsequently.

The methodology usually followed while calculating demand is to assume a constant proportion of steel consumption to the overall GDP, then to the gross fixed capital formation (or the GFCF) and the index of industrial production, or the IIP. The GFCF and IIP are, again, assumed to remain in some constant proportion to the GDP. Then, a growth rate of GDP is assumed (from which, the demand for steel is calculated).[6] The Working Group Report (12th FYP) calculates the elasticity of steel as follows:[7]

Steel elasticities with respect to GDP et al. calculated with data between 2004–05 and 2010–11

With respect to GDP	1.14
With respect to GFCF	0.96
With respect to IIP	0.89

Table 7.6 Growth of the steel-consuming sectors in India

	2013–14	2014–15	2015–16 (April to December)
	In y-o-y percentage		
Consumer durables	−12.2	−12.6	12.4
Manufacturing	−0.8	2.3	3.1

Source: Economic Survey, 2016.

The unexpected slowing down of manufacturing and the mounting debts of infrastructure projects, especially power, roads, railway sidings, warehouses and port renovations, have suppressed the demand for steel, unabashedly.

The data in Table 7.7 shows that demand projections were far too optimistic and not realistic enough. A possible reason was the assumption that the macro indicators would grow rather faster than what had been the case. Browsing through the Economic Survey of 2016, we observe that the GCFC and IIP growth rates have been very disappointing. The GCFC grew at a year-on-year percentage of merely 3.6% in FY 14-15 and by 2.8% in FY 12-13 and dropped by 3.7% in the middle year. The growth in the IIP, year on year, was −0.1% in FY 13-14 and 2.8% in FY 14-15. The consumer durables declined by −12.6% over the previous year, while the growth in capital goods and basic goods was nowhere close to what were envisaged. The growth of the GDP was the worst damper; instead of the predicted 8%, 8.5%, 9% and even 9.5%, the growth was no more than 5.4% to 7.3%. The crash of the macro variables is the real cause for the failure of demand for steel in India.

Presenting the above data in a tabular form, we obtain Table 7.8.

Clearly, the assumption that the GDP will grow anywhere between 8% and 10% was much off the mark.

Table 7.7 Forecast versus reality of the steel demand in India

| Scenarios | *In million tonnes* | | | |
	2011–12	*2012–13*	*2013–14*	*2014–15*
Scenario I with 8% growth in GDP: demand for finished steel including exports	66.5	77.3	85.05	93.6
Scenario II with 8.5% growth in GDP: demand for finished steel including exports	66.5	75.3	84.6	94.1
Actual production of finished steel inclusive of exports	73.42	81.68	87.68	92.16
Apparent consumption	70.92	74.1	73.49	76.99
Exports forecast	3.3	4	5	6
Imports forecast	7	6	5.5	5.5
Exports actual	4.04		6	5.6
Imports actual	6.83		5.5	9.32
Crude steel capacity forecast	81.9	93	104.4	116.2
Crude steel capacity actual	90.87	97.02	102.27	109.85

Source: Working Group Report for the 12th Plan.

Table 7.8 Growth of various macroeconomic variables in India

Variable	2012–13	2013–14	2013–14	2014–15
GDP (2011–12 prices) year on year growth in %	5.6	6.6	7.2	7.6
Gross value added (2011–12 prices) y-o-y growth in %	5.4	6.3	7.1	7.3
IIP in y-o-y %	1.1	−0.1	2.8	3.1
Gross fixed capital y-o-y growth in %		3.4	4.9	5.3

Source: Economic Survey, 2016–17.

Conclusion

The so-called demand failure of the steel industry can be looked upon as demand which did not materialize because it was projected too high to be realistic. The robust growth of demand in the pre-liberalization 1980s in India gave hope to the policy makers and the business experts that in the post-liberalization period, the demand for steel would grow at least by that much, if not by more. Liberalization was supposed to usher in the golden days of everlasting happiness. Unfortunately for India, liberalization that also meant globalization and free markets brought forth more goods, especially steel from countries with higher competitiveness that flooded the Indian markets, killing many local brands; this onslaught affected the steel industry, as well. Hence, supplies increased more than what the economy could absorb, leading to the impression that demand has failed.

Notes

1 deepak.sahu@vccircle.com. Infracircle, 23 June 2016.
2 Economic Survey 2014–15, p. 25, www.thehinducentre.com/multimedia/archive/02324/Economic_Survey_Vo_2324734a.pdf.
3 Ibid.
4 Working Group Report on the Indian Steel Industry for the Twelfth Five Year Plan (2012 to 2017). Ministry of Steel, p. 37, https://mme.iitm.ac.in/shukla/wg_steel2212(1).pdf.
5 Indian Budget official website, http://economictimes.indiatimes.com/news/economy/infrastructure/budget-2016-infrastructure-back-in-focus-with-an-outlay-of-rs-221246-crore/articleshow/51206466.cms.
6 S.P. Pal. *The Long Term of Steel In India*. National Council of Applied Economic Research. Delhi. 1985.
7 Working Group Report on the Indian Steel Industry for the Twelfth Five Year Plan (2012 to 2017). Ministry of Steel, p. 41.

8 The myth of the S curve

Steel is not really a single industry; it consists of mines and minerals, raw material preparation such as oxygen plants, coal gassifiers, coke ovens, blast furnaces, iron pellets and equipment for directly reducing iron. Steel requires the rolling of ingots into various shapes through rolling mills, hot strip mills and cold rolling. Steel needs to be reshaped further into thinner and narrower shapes closer to the final consumers; and these are done through service centres. Steel sheets can be galvanized or coated and painted, for which there are galvanizing, coating and painting lines. Steel needs to transport materials five times its weight; and this requires logistics and transportation. Steel is slow to gestate profitability; and this creates a need for credit and finance. Steel needs an entire army of persons trained as chemical, mechanical, electrical and civil engineers, metallurgists and automatic and instrumentation engineers, as well as experts in thermodynamics, chemistry and biochemistry. Steel needs data managers, IT professionals and trained workers for the furnaces. Steel needs users, designers and consumers (who can buy and use steel in buildings), structures, vehicles, utensils and so on. Steel means large factories, railways, containers, carriers and ports; steel means pollution, emissions and effluents that require technology interventions to control. Steel is, therefore, a collection of industries, rather than being a single entity. No wonder steel is called a sector.

While there is no country in the world which does not consume steel, not every country can produce steel. The production of steel requires the bringing together of money, materials, manpower and markets. Only countries with stable societies, a strong and steady middle class intelligentsia, with a firm and institutionalized banking sector, established trading class and some semblance of infrastructure, at least railways and ports, can hope to produce steel. Steel means putting together a slew of companies: like cement to build the factories and infrastructure, power companies for the supply of power, water supply for the factories (as steel is a water guzzler), and disciplines and institutions to monitor the emissions and effluents out of the steelmaking process (as steel is among the highest polluters in the manufacturing sector). Steel needs institutions to produce metallurgists and engineers, a slew of laboratories for experiments, strong quality control mechanisms to ensure quality of products, equipment suppliers, installation agents and other similar support groups. Not all societies are as complex and organically structured to be able to put together such diverse aspects together to produce steel. The supply constraints of steel are formidable. Steelmaking is so elaborate that most steel plants are located in veritable steel cities, and even those of smaller scale can sprawl over campuses of a hundred acres.

But steel is dependent upon the availability of mineral resources, and while some countries, like Japan, may have no mineral deposits, and yet can be among the top producers of steel, a country like Canada, that is resource intensive, may not be a major steel-producing nation. In the aftermath of the Second World War, the production of steel depended more on technology than upon raw materials; the price of steel used to be the premium of technology. However, in present times, technology is fairly standardized and steel is generally overproduced across the globe; it is not very difficult to produce steel in any country. If it is not the advantage in raw materials or the technology, then the decision whether a country should make or buy its steel must depend on the relative profits of the steel industry. One may say that the location of a steel industry in any country, and its expansion (or contraction) depends on the relative profits that steel earns, compared to the other industries.

Steel is electricity intensive; and much depends upon the level of electricity available in countries. Countries with higher concentrations of population and urban populations help create the demand for steel. Conventionally, it was thought that the steel industry was connected to the level of economic development of a country. Very poor countries could not afford any resources whatsoever to produce steel; but the next rung of the so-called "middle income" countries produced steel to cover their needs of development (like laying down railways, building bridges, setting up factories and erecting apartment homes for people to live in). These countries, the so-called developing countries, need a gush of steel to be able to build up their infrastructure, urbanize societies and lay a strong base for their manufacturing sectors. The middle income countries, or the developing nations, appear to consume and produce more steel. For countries that are in the top levels of economic development, and have put almost every kind of infrastructure in place (and attained the fullest levels of their economic development), namely built all the apartments they needed to build, and bought all the cars they needed to buy; the need for steel appears to have satiated. Very high income countries thus produce less steel. If we plot the countries with low, middle and high incomes, we may obtain a curve which resembles the S. This is the famous S curve that relates steel consumption to the level of economic development in a country.

What is the S curve?

Conventional theories suggest that the demand for steel in a country depends upon its level of economic development, urbanization, population growth, ability to generate electricity and of course, the purchasing power of its people. In present times, such relationships are likely to uncouple, for the world has moved beyond abject poverty, where nations struggled to modernize. Today, much of the primitive states of existence have been addressed and dealt with, and the richest nations are not the ones with the most — miles of railways or high rise buildings and grand cities — but are those with very high profits from IT, banking and finance, or trading; in short, from the non-manufacturing sector. Indeed, the poorer countries are the ones left with the task of manufacturing.

In the past decade, the rise of China has changed the profile of the world; from being a fair spread of manufacturing among the middle income countries, into being peripheries for supply of minerals for China's gigantic appetite for manufacturing. China is most certainly the centre for manufacturing today, with the rest of the world falling over one another to supply raw materials to China. This has actually taken the spirit out of every theory around development of industries as being a crucial step towards modernization. Indeed, countries may well survive out of their mineral wealth, leaving the task of manufacturing to China. This is why there are many countries who should have, under previous times, set up steel industries, but presently, appear to be content with imports and using their mineral wealth to promote such imports of finished products. The whole of central Asia and much of Africa and Latin America are merely raw material suppliers for China. We need to revise our theories: to assess which countries are likely to have a steel industry, and what encourages them to set up their steel businesses. For this, we return to the S curve.

S curve

The countries for which the data on steel production is collected and published by the IISI are roughly eighty in number and have per capita incomes varying between USD 1209 per year for Myanmar to USD 140649 per capita per year for Qatar. These countries are classified into four groups: the poorest are those with per capita income from USD 1000 to 10,000, the second group consists of per capita income from USD 11,000 to 20,000, the third from USD 21,000 to 60,000 and the last consists of those few who are above USD 61,000. The average per capita incomes and the production of steel in the year 2013 (in thousand tonnes) is presented in Table 8.1.

We could plot countries with steel production against their per capita income; per capita income usually reflects the prosperity of nations. We would expect the middle income countries to have bloated steel production, while the lower and the upper income countries would produce less.

Table 8.1 Steel production and per capita income across nations

Per capita income in USD (per person per year)	Average per capita incomes (in USD per year)	Average steel production in 2013 (in thousand tonnes)
1000–10,000	4935	39909
11,000–20,000	15069	8020
21,000–60,000	39596	16957
61,000 and above	104061	3013

Source: Own calculations drawn from Steel Statistics Yearbook, 2014. IISI. Brussels.

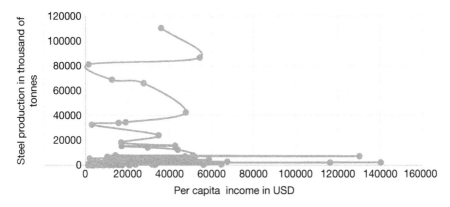

Figure 8.1 The S curve: total steel production and per capita income for all countries

Figure 8.1 emerges as a neat S curve, thus affirming the thesis that steel production is in the form of the S, growing fast for those countries who are still laying their industrial foundation, and dipping down for the segment that seem to have already laid the foundation (and are now in the position of diversifying into other industries). In the third category, steel production rises again, perhaps as these countries emerge as exporters of steel, and in the very high income brackets, steel ceases to be the most profitable industry. This neat model, however, has many exceptions to the trends within each income category, as the figures 8.1, 8.2 and 8.3 show in the curves that are haywire.

Disaggregating steel producing behaviour within each income class

Middle income countries which have fallen to low income and lost steel industry Facilities

In the first category of countries with the lowest per capita income, we have countries that have fallen down into this class due to political upheavals, revolutions and wars. These countries are: Bulgaria, Romania, Moldova and the Ukraine. Known as expert steelmakers, these countries today suffer from dislocations, displacements, loss of assets and partition of lands. These countries have lost their steelmaking facilities. Thailand and Paraguay were robust steel producers, but over time, seem to have given up on making steel. Thailand, of course, diversified its industries and hence, drew out resources and investments from its steel making industries. But, Paraguay is presently focusing more on its natural resources and mineral industries than on its steel industry.

Conventionally low income countries: where the steel is growing

The countries that have emerged as outstanding steelmakers among the lower income countries are: Morocco, in Africa, and Vietnam, in Asia. Morocco is a host to global investors in steel, who use the land of Morocco to produce steel and serve the

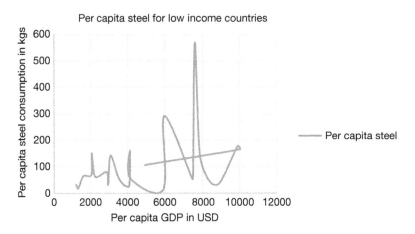

Figure 8.2 Per capita steel consumption and per capita income in low income countries

entire African continent, in which only a few countries produce steel. Nigeria, in Africa, is opening up to global steel capital, along the lines of Morocco. El Salvador and Guatemela, in Central America, are similarly host countries for steelmakers, and they take advantage of the NAFTA integration (and the fact that their currencies are cheaper than the US or the Canadian dollar) and they can operate out of their peripheral lands to supply to NAFTA. Both Vietnam and Philippines enjoy good growth in their steel industries because investments from China, Taiwan, and even South Korea and Singapore and Malaysia are flowing into these countries, so that steel companies get to relocate, literally, into greener pastures. India and China are the biggest stars in Asia, and together with a giant, like Japan, are emerging into a near monopoly of steel, in the world. Bosnia and Herzegovina, in southeast Europe, is perhaps, now attracting the disembodied steel industry of Eastern Europe, and due to heavy investments into reconstruction in this country, steel seems to have found a new home here.

Middle income and declining steel industries

The second class of countries in which steel production appears to be dipping is replete with nations (like Serbia, Latvia, Poland and other east European nations) for whom the steel industry is fast declining. These countries had steel industries geared to local demand, and after a satiation in demand for steel (and the inability to cross the glass ceiling of development further into the levels of the high income countries), the steel industry in these countries is declining due to their demand stagnations.

Middle income growing steel industry

However, in the middle income category, the countries that show promising growth are Albania and Ecuador. Albania is emerging out of the post-Soviet turmoil, and though never a part of the USSR, it was nevertheless its close ally. In the aftermath of the collapse of the Soviet Union, Albania looked towards China for investments in its economy. But, ever since it integrated in NATO in 2009, it seems to have grown closer to Turkish investors. The NATO integration makes Albania a safe haven for much of Turkey's steel investors. The Turkish steel giant, Kurum, moved into Albania to make use of its cheap hydel power, which is also clean. Albania's olive branch to the global steel investor, precisely, lies in the fact that it has developed rich sources of hydro power that it wants to rent out to energy intensive industries; fortuitously, steel is an energy intensive industry.

The story of Ecuador is interesting as well; it was a small steel producer, producing only for its local and domestic use. Importing semis from China, the Ecuadorian steel industry was mostly rerollers. But now, the story has been reversed by Eldeco. Just as Kurum Steel has changed the face of Albania, Eldeco has changed the face of Ecuador. It has set up a large scale electric arc furnace to use the scrap generated in the Americas for making steel. Uruguay and Paraguay have been clearing houses for steel scrap, but they did not care to make steel with the scrap. Ecuador's rise is due to the processing of steel scrap as pencil ingots and billets.

Those with moderate levels of steel industry growth are: Egypt, Cuba and Turkey. Iran is cashing in its natural gas resources and inviting global steel capital. Colombia wants to make use of its excellent quality of coking coal by offering to host steel plants, through the oxygen route with coke oven gas plants.

Rich countries, slowing steel

In the class III countries, prosperity is well established (this includes most of the EU countries, Japan and the USA). These countries are diminishing their steel productions, closing down plants and pulling down factories. Clearly, these countries have developed industries with returns higher than those earned in the steel business, and are moving investments away from this sector. The developed countries seem

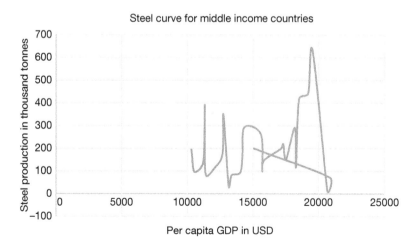

Figure 8.3 Per capita GDP and steel production in middle income countries

to have exhausted their appetite in consuming steel; they have literally had enough, and no longer see a point in adding capacity.

Rich countries, growing steel

The exceptions to this trend are: Croatia, Saudi Arabia and surprisingly, Switzerland. Both Croatia and Switzerland have increased their steel capacities by investing heavily into specialized stainless steel for very high value-added applications. Saudi Arabia intends to use its cheap natural gas, long coastline, geographical fortune (in being literally, in the centre of the world) and its well-developed logistics, to be able to invest in steel production and its exports. Saudi Arabia has received bounties from China (in the form of investments in the steel sector) and now, is likely to pick up the strands from where the overheated steel industry of China would cool off. Among the richest countries of the world, the UAE and Qatar are enthusiastically adding steelmaking capacities (to perhaps, develop steel as a commodity, which will become handy in hedging, since oil prices are dropping). In this, the intentions of the last mentioned countries are similar to those of Saudi Arabia.

The growth of steel in Portugal is interesting as well; it appears that the cooling off of steel in Spain, Italy, France and even Poland, is not affecting Portugal. Portugal is producing an array of steel products (including mild and stainless steel, as well as alloy and coated steel) and appears to be dominated by an array of service centres and finishing lines receiving semis from all over Europe. Portugal is looking towards export of finished products into Africa, especially North Africa. Investing heavily into Tunisia, Portuguese investors are trying to develop the country as a clearing house for steel.

Thus, while on the whole, the S curve does exist; it is only a law of averages: one cannot draw conclusions out of the S curve of possible connections between steel production and the level of prosperity of a country.

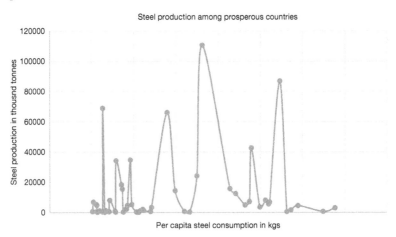

Figure 8.4 Steel production and per capita income among prosperous countries

Correlations and disaggregations

The commonly accepted levels of economic development are per capita income, per head consumption of electricity, percentage of population living in urban areas and density of population. We have presented some correlations between steel production of a country, per capita steel consumption and various other indicators, like urbanization, per capita income and consumption of electricity, only to come to no real conclusions. The correlations among these indicators of development and steel production appear to be very weak (Table 8.2a). The only worthwhile relationship exists between the level of electricity consumption and per capita income, at 0.73. There appears to be some connection between per capita consumption of steel and electricity as well, at 0.60. Some amount of correlation exists between urbanization and prosperity. Thus, while urbanization and electricity and prosperity of citizens are connected, these have little to do with steel. These are very surprising results, and tell us that one cannot draw definitive conclusions about steel production, or steel consumption as related to a country's level of economic development.

Table 8.2a Correlations among the various development indicators: all countries

Correlations	Per capita steel use (in kgs)	Electricity consumption (in kwh per hour)	% of population in urban areas	Population density (per square km)	Per capita income (in USD)	Steel production (in thousand tonnes)
Per capita steel consumption (in kgs)	1	0.59	0.39	0.43	0.43	0.24
Per capita electricity consumption	0.59	1	0.50	0.10	0.73	0.01
Urban population as % of all population	0.39	0.5	1	0.18	0.50	−0.04
Population density (per sq km)	0.43	0.1	0.18	1.00	0.14	−0.01
Per capita income (in USD)	0.43	0.73	0.5	0.14	1.00	−0.06
Steel production (in thousand tonnes)	0.24	0.01	−0.04	−0.01	−0.06	1

Source: Obtained from Steel Statistical Year Book, 2013 and World Development Indicators, World Bank.

Table 8.2b Correlations between steel production and other indicators disaggegated as per income class of countries

Income class of countries	Per capita income (in USD)	Per capita steel use (in kgs)	Electricity consumption (in kwh per head)	Percentage of urban population	Population density (persons per sq km)	Growth of steel (in %)
I	0.17	0.82	0.32	0.07	0.02	−0.04
II	0.04	0.36	0.36	0.17	−0.20	−0.06
III	0.08	0.37	0.23	0.14	−0.09	−0.08
IV	0.48	−0.28	−0.92	−0.71	−0.23	−0.04

Note: The classes are in ascending order.
Source: Ibid.

If we disaggregate our data set into income classes, and then look for connections between the level of prosperity and steel industry, we get an erratic picture (Table 8.2b). While the correlations of indicators of development and steel production are weak throughout, the relationship of the steel industry and economic development appear to be different, for different disaggregated classes of countries.

For the poorest countries, steel production is related to the per capita steel consumption, which is nothing but the total production of steel divided by population.

Steel production appears to be fairly independent of the indicators of development for every other class of country (except for the super-rich, where correlations are stronger but negative). Among the richest, steel production is negatively correlated to urbanization and electricity consumption, showing that these are satiated countries who have consumed all the steel that they need to, and are now dismantling their facilities.

The puzzle of low correlations of steel with indicators of economic development

Steel is consumed through buildings, bridges, consumer durables, automobiles and so on; steel, therefore, means assets; and the levels of assets in the society depends on a host of things, among them, the ratio of current income to the assets in the society. In societies where the assets held are many times the current income, such societies have a lower proclivity to acquire newer assets; hence, such societies may consume less steel. This means that societies with high inequality tend to consume less steel, even if they are in the middle income zone and are developing; however, if such societies invest in public investments, then they may consume steel, despite high inequalities and low levels of asset penetration.

Primitive societies are egalitarian and have little need to accumulate assets; such societies also consume less steel. It is only societies that are growing with hunger for assets that would consume steel. Societies, therefore, must be growing; they must already have enough income (in order to set a part of that aside for building up assets) and the growth in income must be widespread and generate enough well-distributed surplus for people to build assets up. The price of assets must not be too high for people to be deterred from purchases. The consumption of steel must be linked to the growth of assets of the society, which depends more upon the growth of income; the distribution of that growth and the price of assets, relative to the price of the basket of consumables.

The production of steel, on the other hand, depends upon how much capital a society can put together to invest in steel, and this, in turn, depends upon the strength of the banking institutions, the strength of government planning, the control over markets, and the ability to provide platforms for information dissemination about supply, demand and prices of steel items. Without such mechanisms, nations cannot put together the enormous variety and quantity of resources needed to manufacture steel.

Conclusion

The immediate fact that strikes us rather strongly is that steel production cannot be predicted from its related variables (such as electricity consumption, urbanization, population growth and others). The relationship of steel production to macro-economic variables, like urbanization and population growth, appear to be rather weak. There is no guarantee that a rich country will produce steel and a poorer nation will not do so. Extending this argument, it is difficult to predict, or even forecast, the production of steel. The only hope for any prediction, perhaps, lies in the understanding that, while the production of steel depends upon the ability of the society to put together resources, knowledge, markets and talent, steel consumption depends more on the asset acquisition behavior of societies, in which lower levels of inequality, combined with high economic growth, create opportunities for increase in steel consumption. The Indian policy makers are concerned about ways and means to increase the consumption of steel in India; to promote the consumption of steel one must address the asset accumulating behaviour of the society (by which it buys its cars, washing machines, apartment homes, factories, flyovers and shopping malls).

Appendix I: correlations among steel production and the various macro economic variables and development indicators of countries in income classes

Table 8A.1 Class I countries with per capita annual income USD >1000 to <10,000

Country	Per capita income (in USD)	Steel production (in thousand tonnes)	Per capita steel use (in kgs)	Electricity consumption (in kwh per hour)	% of population in urban areas	Population density (per square km)
Year	2011–2015	2013	2013	2011–2015	2011–2015	2011–2016
Myanmar	1204	30	32	151	34	82
Pakistan	1316	972	19	457	38	240

(continued)

Table 8A.1 Continued

Country	Per capita income (in USD)	Steel production (in thousand tonnes)	Per capita steel use (in kgs)	Electricity consumption (in kwh per hour)	% of population in urban areas	Population density (per square km)
India	1582	81299	64	698	32	436
Uzbekistan	2037	746	70	1605	36	72
Vietnam	2052	5474	151	1099	33	293
Moldova	2239	190	63	1515	45	124
Philippines	2873	1308	80	651	44	332
Kenya	2954	20	32	160	25	79
Ukraine	3083	32771	142	3641	69	76
Indonesia	3492	2644	62	681	53	140
Sri Lanka	3819	30	30	491	18	329
Ghana	4082	25	29	346	53	118
Mongolia	4129	40	161	1495	71	2
North Korea	4150	1250	55	657	61	208
Nigeria	5911	100	14	156	47	195
Thailand	5977	3579	291	2305	49	133
Guatemela	7454	385	53	531	51	149
Morocco	7491	558	59	875	60	76
China	7590	821990	568	3298	54	145
Bulgaria	7851	523	149.7	4762	74	67
El Salvador	8351	118	48	857	66	295
Paraguay	8911	45	38	1283	59	16
Bosnia Herzegovina	9892	722	178	3276	40	75
Romania	9997	2985	165.1	2604	54	87
Average	**4934.88**	**39908.50**	**106.41**	**1399.75**	**48.58**	**157.04**
Slope		0.00	7.83	1.03	93.07	-8.67
Correlations		0.17	0.33	0.46	0.48	-0.34

Source: Table derived from Steel Statistical Yearbook, 2014.

Table 8A.2 Class II countries with per capita annual income USD >10,000 to < 21,000

Country	Per capita income	Steel production (in thousand tonnes)	Per capita steel use (in kgs)	Electricity consumption (in kwh per hour)	% of population in urban areas	Population density (per square km)
Year	2011–2015	2013	2013	2011–2015	2011–2015	2011–2016
Albania	10305	550	195	248	56	48
Egypt	10530	6754	96	1700	43	90
Argentina	11199	5186	139	2901	87	16
Malaysia	11307	4693	392	4114	74	91
Ecuador	11318	570	130	1219	64	64
Tunisia	11436	150	78	1411	67	71
Peru	11989	1069	108	1242	78	24
Serbia	12660	396	174	4387	55	82
Russia	12735	68856	349	6617	74	9
Macedonia	13142	100	33	3690	57	82
Colombia	13357	1236	81	1121	76	43
Hungary	14029	583	93.4	3919	71	109
Algeria	14193	440	169	1236	70	16
Poland	14343	7950	293.3	3899	61	124
Libya	15600	712	262	4707	78	4
Latvia	15719	198	103.1	3588	67	32
Brazil	15838	34163	147	2394	85	25
Mexico	17108	18208	198	2074	79	65
Iran	17303	15422	219	2762	73	48
Azerbaijan	17516	173	152	2053	54	115
Belarus	18185	2245	291	3698	76	47
Venezuela	18276	2139	117	3336	89	35
Slovak	18501	4511	415.2	5138	54	113
Turkey	19200	34654	442	2790	73	99

(continued)

Table 8A.2 Continued

Country	Per capita income	Steel production (in thousand tonnes)	Per capita steel use (in kgs)	Electricity consumption (in kwh per hour)	% of population in urban areas	Population density (per square km)
Czech Republic	19530	5171	630.3	6305	73	136
Cuba	20661	322	14	1322	77	107
Uruguay	20884	91	71	2808	95	20
Average	**15069.04**	**8020.07**	**199.71**	**2988.11**	**70.59**	**63.52**
Slope		0.01	5.63	0.49	103.73	16.32
Correlations		0.13	0.49	0.38	0.25	0.24

Source: Ibid.

Table 8A.3 Class III countries with per capita annual income USD >21,000 to <60,000

Country	Per capita income	Steel production (in thousand tonnes)	Per capita steel use (in kgs)	Electricity consumption (in kwh per hour)	% of population in urban areas	Population density (per square km)
Year	2011-2015	2013	2013	2011-2015	2011-2015	2011-2016
Croatia	21210	135	156	3819	59	76
Greece	21498	1030	107.5	5511	78	85
Portugal	22132	2050	234.4	4736	63	114
Chile	22346	1323	179	3590	89	24
Slovenia	23999	608	473.3	6778	50	102
Kazakhstan	24228	3275	256	5085	53	6
South Korea	27905	66061	1105	10162	62	517
Spain	29767	14252	241	5573	79	93
Trinidad and Tobago	31967	616	246	6390	9	264
Israel	33230	300	311	7189	92	380
Italy	34909	24080	377.2	5398	69	209

Table 8A.3 Continued

Country	Per capita income	Steel production (in thousand tonnes)	Per capita steel use (in kgs)	Electricity consumption (in kwh per hour)	% of population in urban areas	Population density (per square km)
Japan	36194	110595	561	7841	93	349
France	42733	15685	228.4	7344	79	121
Canada	44057	12415	448	16168	82	4
United Kingdom	46332	4858	153.4	5452	82	267
Belgium	47353	7093	391.3	7987	98	371
Germany	47832	42645	507.3	7270	75	232
Finland	49834	3517	348.4	15687	84	18
Austria	51191	7953	475.6	8507	66	103
Saudi Arabia	51925	5471	445	8405	83	14
Netherlands	52172	6713	236.6	6871	90	501
United States	54630	86878	334	13240	81	35
Singapore	56285	434	1019	8657	100	7736
Switzerland	57236	1530	381	7886	74	207
Sweden	58939	4404	410	14290	86	24
Average	**39596.16**	**16956.84**	**385.016**	**7993.44**	**75.04**	**474.08**
Slope		**0.03**	**14.10**	**2.24**	**302.67**	**2.31**
Correlations		**0.08**	**0.26**	**0.60**	**0.45**	**0.27**

Source: Ibid.

Table 8A.4 Class IV countries with per capita annual income USD >60,000

	Per capita income	Steel production (in thousand tonnes)	Per capita steel use (in kgs)	Electricity consumption (in kwh per hour)	% of population in urban areas	Population density (per square km)
Year	2011–2015	2013	2013	2011–2015	2011–2015	2011–2016
Norway	64856	605	205	23658	80	14
UAE	67674	2878	861	10463	85	109

(continued)

Table 8A.4 Continued

	Per capita income	Steel production (in thousand tonnes)	Per capita steel use (in kgs)	Electricity consumption (in kwh per hour)	% of population in urban areas	Population density (per square km)
Luxembourg	116664	2090	304	14696	90	215
South Africa	130462	7254	123	4405	64	46
Qatar	140649	2236	994	16183	99	187
Average	**104061**	**3012.6**	**497.4**	**13881**	**83.6**	**114.2**
Slope		**6.78**	**6.36**	**−2.04**	**320.22**	**207.13**
Correlations		**0.48**	**0.07**	**−0.41**	**0.12**	**0.51**

Source: Ibid.

9 The metallic balance of steel

Steel is a material-intensive substance. A tonne of steel consumes no less than 1.6 tonnes of iron ore, another 1.6 tonnes of coal as direct energy, carbon and electricity, about another half a tonne of fluxes, scrap and other metallic substances. This makes steel consume about four times its weight in raw materials. Iron ore is the prime material that the steel industry consumes. Rich sources of iron deposits constitute a major source of advantage for a steel plant, and in the steel-producing countries where iron ore is found, steel plants often choose to be near the sources of iron. But, the United Kingdom, which was the founding nation of industrial revolution and of steel production, and Japan, often known as the pinnacle of modern industrialization, do not have any source of iron ore. China, for a long time, extracted and exported iron ore at a rate many times more than its steel production; South Africa, Australia, Canada, the Ukraine and Brazil produce more iron ore for others to use than what they would keep for their own steel industries. Whether one would want to produce steel out of the iron ore available in their territories, or would like to export them out to steel-producing countries, and whether one would like to produce steel, despite the fact that most of the raw materials will have to be imported, are important elements for consideration while drafting steel policies.

The metallic imbalances of steel

Steel can be made directly out of iron ore by the integrated steel plants, or the primary producers in oxygen furnaces, or by melting scrap and iron derivatives in electric furnaces known as electric steelmakers, or secondary producers. Iron ore is also made by pig iron producers, and the producers of directly reduced iron, or DRI. DRI is absorbed in the processing of crude steel, while pig iron is sold as merchant pig (and used in electric furnaces as well as to further absorb in steel production). The overall requirements of iron ore, therefore, may be considered from the multiplication of crude steel figures with the factor of iron ore, which is 1.6.

Three kinds of metallic material

Steel uses three kinds of metallic materials: iron ore, which is used in blast furnaces of large scale steel plants using the oxygen route; directly reduced iron, or

DRI, which is iron ore freed from its oxides in solid state; and steel scrap. The last two mentioned are used in electric furnaces. Conventionally, DRI could at best constitute 50% of the feed in electric arc furnace, the other half being steel scrap. But in India, the induction furnaces can use as much as 90% of its feed in the form as DRI. The relative prices of the metallic materials may determine the technology choice of promoters of steel companies of the steelmaking route they would choose.

In Figure 9.1 and Table 9.1, the price of iron ore seems to have had the steepest downward slide while the price of scrap seems to have held on. If 1.6 times iron ore is equal to 1.1 tonne of steel scrap, and also to DRI, then, as per the prices in January 2015, iron ore should be $54.5 x 1.6 = $87.2 per tonne of iron ore, while steel scrap by the same measure cost $315 x 1.1 = $346.5. Scrap is costlier. DRI should cost as much as scrap. The oxygen steelmakers would be very well off, as compared to those who would use the electric steel route. Companies would still prefer to go for the extraction of iron ore with high ferrous content, lumpy in size and conventionally used for the blast furnaces. Innovations in ore beneficiation and the DRI may slow down.

Presented in Table 9.2 is metallic balance in India for two years, 2008 and 2014. Both years are calendar years, and the data is extracted from the Steel Statistical Yearbook, IISI, for uniformity.

India has generally viewed itself as a country with surplus iron ore, and yet, the latest figures for 2014 show that it has become iron ore deficient, as well. This is perhaps, because of the rapid rise of the DRI industry between 2008 and 2014, as well as the Chinese imports of iron ore. The deficiency in iron ore has brought about the need to consider the award of mining leases all over again, on the one hand, but, on the other, has led to restrictions on the export of iron ore through the imposition of a (as high as) 30% export tax; though recently, the duties have been somewhat scaled down. The policy makers, who had hitherto encouraged the DRI

Table 9.1 Price spreads of raw materials for steelmaking

Raw materials	Unit	Value as of 30 December 2014	Value as of 30 January 2015	Decline in %
Sponge iron	Rs/tonne	23800	22600	−5.04
Iron ore 63.5% Fe	USD/tonne	60.5	54.5	−9.92
Shredded scrap	USD/tonne	330	315	−4.54
Coal	USD/tonne	64	62	−3.33
Billet	Rs/tonne	32300	31000	−4.03

Note: Coal is Australian Coal, 6300 Kcal/tonne.
Source: Oreteam, February 2015.

Table 9.2 Iron ore and scrap balance in India

In thousand tonnes	2008	2014
Total crude steel produced	57791	87292
Crude steel through oxygen converters	22151	37045
Requirement of iron ore in oxygen steel assuming that 90% of feed material is iron ore	83219.04	125700.5
Production of DRI	21200	20366
Iron ore requirement for DRI assuming that 1.6 times iron ore is needed for a unit of DRI	33920	32585.6
Total iron ore required	117139	158286.1
Iron ore produced in the country	223000	129800
Iron ore exported	101404	9844
Iron ore imported	600	7413
Iron ore available	122196	127369
Iron ore available less iron ore needed/surplus	5056.96	-30917.1
Crude steel through electric furnaces	35223	50211
Use of scrap at 10% of electric steel at 1.1 times the unit of steel produced	3875	5523
Scrap exported	0	0
Scrap imported	4579	5699
Surplus scrap	704	176

Source: Own calculations and Steel Statistical Yearbook, 2015, IISI, Brussels.

industry to add value to iron ore found in the country, are now in no mood to encourage this industry, alleging that it pollutes the environment and should be shut down, especially, as it serves the low end induction furnaces. But, fresh mining leases are also held at ransom due to the problems of rampant abrogation of mining laws, especially when Chinese buying was buoyant. Without a consistent

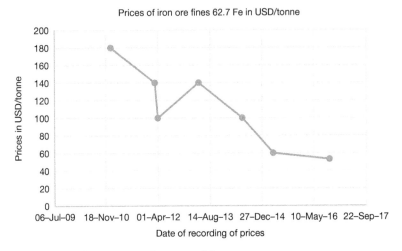

Figure 9.1 Declining prices of raw materials

Source: Courtesy of www.Infomine.com

mining policy in view, and without a readymade calculation of whether to hand over the iron ore mines to steel producers (or to invite specialized dedicated mining companies on board), India may have to bear the deficiency in iron ore availability in the near term.

DRI (directly reduced iron) rising

DRI is a derivative of iron reduced from iron ore in the presence of oxygen, but without melting the iron ore as it is done in blast furnaces. Instead of the molten iron in the form of hot metal, DRI is dry, though in most cases, vulnerable to exposure to air in normal temperatures. The magic of DRI is that it can be used in electric arc furnaces, as a supplement of steel scrap, but also wholly by itself, as Indian manufacturers have shown to the world. India is the world's largest manufacturer of the DRI, producing 20 million tonnes annually, compared to the world production of some 80 million tonnes. Though India manufactures DRI through its high ferrous containing haematite ore, for most of the world, especially Nordic Europe and the CIS and the Middle East, DRI is manufactured out of iron pellets, which are, again, sifted and sieved out of inferior iron ore (having substantially lower ferrous content). Most of the world's DRI is made out of beneficiated ore. While DRI is a polluting industry, when its emissions and effluents are controlled, DRI can be ecologically sustainable only because it makes use of the ore that is usually discarded for being low in iron content by steel producers. Beneficiated iron ore is closely connected to the DRI industry, and clearly, countries, like Sweden, Russia, Finland, the USA and most importantly, the Middle East, are concentrating on the manufacture of DRI.

Scrap versus DRI

DRI, rather than the iron ore, is likely to emerge as the leading raw material for non-EU countries and for South America, Africa and the Middle East. Among these, only Europe may be comfortable in steel scrap, but for the rest of the world, which is largely developing, scrap may be difficult to obtain, and for such regions, DRI will be the material of the future; although, scrap will continue to dominate the market, since it is used almost six times as much as DRI as a raw material. The issue of DRI versus steel scrap becomes important, in terms of investments into the future; while scrap is largely the domain of traders (as it is a quick-moving commodity, based on immediate transactions), DRI needs to be mined, beneficiated and manufactured and involves long-term investments. Besides, DRI cannot be really transshipped, except in the form of the hot briquetted iron, or HBI, which is made out of natural gas, instead of coal. The chemical composition of the briquetted iron made out of natural gas is more stable than those made out of coal; and shipment rules allow the former to be on board. But, HBI made out of natural gas has the problem of high carbon content, which coal-based DRI does not have, which makes the latter, therefore, more suitable for the manufacture of steel. High investments and the difficulties of transportation may mean that the DRI is developed for local industry.

The imminent fall of the world leader, India, in the DRI industry

The DRI industry in India operates with a large base of smaller producers. The DRI makers in India have small rotary kilns and use coal, both as a source of energy, as well as a source of carbon, and use the locally available hematite ore as input. Producing close to 20 million tonnes, DRI supports a quarter of the crude steel capacities in India. However, the Chinese's buying of iron ore at astronomical prices made the sale of iron ore lucrative, while production of DRI is less economically attractive. DRI producers undertook the sale of ore and starved their own plants; in this scenario, three different groups, namely the mine owners without DRI plants, the mine owners with DRI plants and the DRI plants without iron ore mines, were involved. The DRI industry crashed, reverting the electric furnace industry of India back to its dependence on scrap, most of which is imported. The use of DRI as a cheaper alternative to scrap appears to be less available to the electric arc furnaces, and clearly, this has led to a retardation of the sector.

On the other hand, many Indian companies, like Bhushan Steel, are migrating to the Middle East for access to cheap shale gas, and setting up DRI units by importing low grade magnetite from European neighbours. Clearly, the availability of cheap shale gas, wherever found, has created a new avenue for the DRI industry. DRI, which is made out of natural gas, is known as HBI, which, because of a more stable chemistry, is allowed to travel on seafaring vessels, whereas DRI made out of coal is not. The latter is vulnerable to exposure to air and water, and hence, is not fit for shipment. The shift towards gas-based HBI is commercially better and is more lucrative for Sogo Sasha–like operations.

The Sogo Sasha: Japanese methods for accessing raw materials

Japan, which does not have iron ore mines, instead of curtailing the production of steel, in fact, expanded it further. Steel production in Japan maybe did not grow within its own political boundaries, but its investments spread far and wide across China, South Korea, Middle East and even, Africa. The Japanese investments followed those firms who either had their own mines or could bid for mines and hence, in an indirect manner, the Japanese firms were bidding for mines. In India, Nippon Steel invested in Bhushan and Uttam Galva, both of which bid for mines; while Bhushan lost to Essar for an iron ore mine in Odisha, Uttam Galva succeeded in obtaining a mine in Karnataka from the Brahmani group. Posco, a South Korean firm wholly set up by Nippon Steel, wanted to set up an integrated steel plant, only on the hope of getting a captive iron ore mine through it; what was even interesting is that Posco planned to export the hematite ore out of India and import magnetite ore from Brazil.

Mitsui & Company's operations are even more interesting. Most iron ore–exporting countries like Australia and those in Latin America have opened up their mines to Japanese companies, most prominently, Mitsui & Company, for they are the ones who have the funds. Mitsui procures iron ore from Australia and Latin America, brings them to ports in Canada and the United States, channelizes them across the world and collects money through Singapore, to settle accounts. The iron ore trade runs on the concept of the "Sogo Sosha", or networked commodity trading companies.[1] A Marubeni Research Centre paper[2] clearly traces out the path of the Japanese trading ventures in which sourcing, clearing, distribution and finances are in spread out locations. This helps companies to access raw materials, finances, logistics and markets across the globe in the most optimal manner.

The two paths in India to material security

India is caught between integrated steel producers and the smaller electric furnaces once more, through the issue of raw materials. The policy makers are in a dilemma on whether to secure material balance by preserving iron ore only for domestic steel production, or whether to allow its free exports. They also have to consider whether to promote the DRI segment, which is emerging as the next generation of raw materials, or provide only iron ore to the blast furnaces, and whether to allow captive mines or merchant mining. Decisions that allow captive mines and reservation of iron ore for the integrated mills (and insist on the use of iron ore only for indigenous production) usually fatten up debts of companies, as these strategies tend to lower returns on investments in mining. On the other hand, freer exports of iron ore, merchant mining and dissociating iron ore from mere steel production (and engaging it with the newer technologies of iron ore beneficiation and direct reduction) may circulate more money in the economy, paving the path for a scaled-up raw material business.

The world over, steel industries are splitting away from their iron ore businesses; the steel industries in Canada and Australia have, over the years, concentrated on the mineral business and let steel production slide, leaving us with electric furnaces for alloy steel and an array of processors for the manufacture of machinery and sophisticated engineering products. The split down the middle separating raw materials from steel production is perhaps the work of overcapacity, and the increase in demand for iron ore, both fallouts of the mammoth expansion of the Chinese steel industry. While the overcapacity, on the one hand, depressed steel prices, forcing mergers and acquisitions, production outsourcing and intra-industry trade, the increase in demand for raw materials created spaces for investing into technologies of beneficiation, direct reduction and so on. The Japanese style of operations has revealed that raw material security is no longer a matter of owning captive mines, but intelligently combining investments, technology and trade in iron ore.

Conclusions: the key to security is raw material switch

A modern steel policy must be concerned with raw material security of the steel industry, but understand that the parameters of that raw material security are changing. Raw material security is, perhaps, better attained by addressing mining, iron ore beneficiation, direct reduction and pelletization as distinct economic activities. Price continues to be a deciding factor in raw material security, so much so, that raw material prices tend to determine the choice of technology for producing steel. Lower prices of iron ore may encourage the development of the oxygen furnaces, while the lower prices of steel scrap may encourage the setting up of electric furnaces. DRI occupies a space in between, for it can be used both in the blast furnaces as well as in the electric furnaces, and the challenge is to orient furnaces to be able to able to accept a flexible combination of raw materials; indeed, furnace design will constitute a major innovation, in the days to come. With the imminent separation of raw materials and the steel business, steel will get to work with a variety of raw materials, sourced across different mines and geographies. Technologies will focus on creating uniform compositions of raw materials through beneficiation and blending.

Notes

1　What Does a Sogo Sosha Do? Mitsui and Co. Ltd. www.mitsui.com/jp/en/sogoshosha/.
2　Sogo Sosha – An Insider's Perspective. Marubeni Research Centre. 2013. www.marubeni. com/research/report/industry/japan/data/shoshaexp2.pdf.

10 The bad loans of the steel industry

What do the NPAs really tell?

Business Standard reported on 11 August 2015, that in the preceding five years, bank loans to the steel sector had grown by 21% with the banks' exposure to the steel sector, standing at Rs 3 lakh crore.[1] Of this, nearly 4% to 9% are bad loans. Of this, nearly 86% of the loans are with companies that are badly stressed.[2] On 25 March 2016, *Times of India* reported that Rs 50,000 crores of loans to the steel industry was on the verge of turning bad.[3] Nearly a year ago, the RBI had issued a warning that five out of the ten top private steel-producing companies could turn into loss making mammoths. The bad assets of banks due to the exposure to the steel industry constitutes more than 10% of all bad assets while the total exposure of steel to all loans is about 4.5%. Along with power, steel is the worst performing industry in India (Table 10.1).[4]

Case study of Uttam Galva

What is it that makes the steel industry so poor, in terms of investments and loans? In order to get an idea of the steel sector in India, we turn to the story of Uttam Galva, a Maharashtra-based firm for manufacturing high quality cold rolled steel. On 18 November 2015, *Business Standard* reported that Uttam Galva was to acquire stakes in the ailing Lloyds steel, an electric arc furnace–based company, which manufactured flat steels out of the pig iron manufactured by Uttam Galva.[5]

The company pumped Rs 380 crores to rev up Lloyds' capabilities and decided to turn the ailing company around. In the previous year, 2014, Uttam Galva had acquired Brahmani mines and pellets from the mining baron G. Janardhan Reddy.[6] The expenditure was Rs 285 crores. It was a company that was now integrated with mines, iron making facilities, electric furnaces and end products, flats. Yet, the company failed. *Businessline* reported on 1 July 2016, that the company had reported a consolidated loss of Rs 1555 crores against a mild profit of Rs 21 crores in the previous year.[7] The news report suggests that despite such integration, the company incurred heavy losses on account of repeated protection offered to the HR coil segment of the country. The basic business of Uttam Galva was the import of HR coils and the manufacture and export of galvanized coils, and with the slew of protectionist measures (such as safeguards and the Minimum Import Price), the company margins crashed.

Table 10.1 Weight of NPAs due to the steel industry in India

Banks' exposure to steel	Rs 3 lakh crores
Steel loans that are stressed to total loans to steel companies	27%
Steel's share in total advances to all industries	4.7%
Share of steel in total restructured loans to all industries	14%
Share of steel in NPAs in all sectors	6%
Share of steel sector in restructured standard advances to all sectors	19.6%

Source: http://timesofindia.indiatimes.com/business/india-business/Steel-loans-worth-50k-cr-may-turn-bad-in-few-months/articleshow/51545264.cms. 12 August 2016.

The Miglani family, who were the owners of Shree Uttam Steel and Power, have invested a sum of Rs 11,156 crores to float Uttam Galva, a joint venture of their existing company, with the Korean giant, POSCO. Uttam Galva will set up a 3 million tonne steel in Maharashtra to make hot rolled coils.[8] With such a huge spread of investments, the company has accumulated bad debts with its bank, namely the State Bank of India. The bankers have directed the company to infuse fresh money by going for a public issue, and strangely stocks have soared. In short, this is the real story of the bad loans. Investments are directed towards the acquisition of land, mines and assets. The banks have issued loans, not so much on the merit of the steel market, for were they to consider the dynamics and potential of steel markets, it would be immediately evident to them that markets hold little worth in today's day and age of overcapacity; indeed, the loans were directed towards the asset-holding pattern of the company, in relation to mines and land.

The above reason, which is to say that the bad debts of the companies are due to their acquisition of land assets, is also the reason for diversion of funds. As Uttam Galva had investments of Rs 660 crores in integrating production from iron ore to steel mill products, how was it that it managed to incur losses to the tune of Rs 1555 crores, which is twice the amount of its investments? Why is it that the integration did nothing whatsoever towards achieving excellence in steelmaking? Why did the company still need to import hot rolled coils? What were the facilities in Lloyds Steel used for, if not to manufacture HR coils? If the Uttam Galva–Brahmani mines and pellets and Lloyds Steel are already an integrated circuit for steelmaking, then why go for yet another 3 million tonne steel plant with Posco steel especially in the face of losses of such a staggering amount of over Rs 1500 crores? None of the above makes any sense to an economist. Indeed, the stock prices of Uttam Galva have jumped at the news of the sale of its assets.[9]

The cases of Essar Steel and Bhushan Steel: selling assets to buy assets

The story of Uttam Galva is repeated in the following companies, as well. Shashi and Ravi Ruia's Essar group has gross debt of Rs 1,01,461 crore. The group is looking to sell about a 50% stake of its family silver, i.e., Essar Oil's 20mtpa (million tonnes per annum) Vadinar refinery, for Rs 25,000 crore. It also plans to bring in a financial partner for its 10mtpa steel business that, currently, has a debt of Rs 40,000 crore; a 49% stake in the steel facility will be valued at about Rs 25,000 crore. The debt-laden group is also looking to sell a stake in its ports business. Essar Steel and Essar Oil each account for one-third of the group debt, and Essar Power one-fifth.[10] Indeed, in the face of such mounting debts, Essar Steel has bought an iron ore mine in Odisha. Bhushan Steel, yet another company with bad debts, was also a contender for the iron ore asset. Clearly then bad loans are not due to nonperformance but for the acquisition of assets. Banks can always auction such assets through asset reconstruction companies and recover money.[11]

Case study of the Lanco Group

The Lanco Group has debts of Rs 47,102 crore. It completed the sale of its Udupi plant in FY16 for Rs 6,300 crore (15% of FY15 debt). Debt levels have continued to rise, up 6% in FY15. The group plans to sell power assets worth Rs 25,000 crore to de-leverage its balance sheet and retire debts of about Rs 18,000 crore. It is also planning to sell a one-third stake in the Australian coal mine it acquired in 2011 for $750 million.[12] Lanco Industries Limited (LIL) was incorporated on 1 November 1991 by the Lanco Group of Companies to manufacture pig iron using Korf (German) technology and cement. The unit is located at Rachagunneri Village on Tirupathi–Srikalahasthi road which is about 30 km from Tirupathi and 10 km from Srikalahasthi. The installed capacity of pig iron was 90,000 TPA with a similar capacity of 90,000 TPA for cement. The operation of the cement unit of the company was suspended for various reasons and the unit was reengineered for producing a different product mix with potential in south India.

As a forward integration project for adding value to the pig iron manufactured by the company, LIL floated another company named Lanco Kalahasthi Castings Limited (LKCL) on 4 March 1997 to manufacture iron castings and spun pipes in the same campus of the company with an annual capacity of 40,000 TPA and 35,700 TPA, respectively.

At a time when the company was exploring a financial and technical strategic alliance with an Indian/foreign partner, Electrosteel Castings Limited was also looking for additional capacities for producing spun pipes. Considering the synergies involved, Lanco Industries Limited entered into a strategic alliance partnership during December 2002 with Electrosteel Castings Limited (ECL), Kolkata, a leading manufacturer of CI, pipes and DI pipes. This was a win–win situation for both

LIL and ECL. After the takeover, a financial re-engineering and re-structuring of LIL was undertaken by ECL.[13] Electrosteel Castings Limited today is among the top loan defaulters.[14]

Case study of Visa Steel and Power

In FY15, Visa reported a loss of Rs 273 crore on the back of Rs 1,260 crore in net revenues. The finance costs more than doubled to Rs 229 crore and according to Bloomberg data, the gross debt stood at Rs 3,094 crore, up 10.5% over FY14. Visa's borrowings of around Rs 3,000 crore were restructured under the corporate debt restructuring (CDR) mechanism in FY13. In September last year, lenders decided to convert a large portion of debt into equity using the SDR (Strategic Debt Restructuring) scheme by which the Reserve Bank of India allows banks to convert a part of their outstanding loans into equity. Hudco has declared Visa Steel an NPA. Other lenders to Visa Steel are Bank of Baroda (BoB), Punjab National Bank (PNB), Bank of India (BoI), Canara Bank and a few banks from the SBI Group and Syndicate Bank. According to the FY15 annual report, the company plans to expand capacity from 0.5 million tonne per annum (TPA) to 1 million TPA special steel at Kalinganagar in Odisha. The 0.5 million TPA special steel business includes production of hot metal, pig iron and other materials for supply to the automobile, construction, infrastructure, engineering, railway and defense sectors.[15]

What does one make out of the above case studies?

One observes that the bad loans of the steel companies as described above have emanated out of the attempts of stand-alone steel plants to expand capacities to over a million tonnes and acquire facilities and iron ore mines like the integrated steel plants. As stand-alone plants the defaulting steel facilities were all doing well but as they combine forces and strive to become integrated steel mills they fall into a debt trap. The idea behind integration is to be able to have security of raw materials and intermediate inputs but in effect these plants in their combined forces seem to have done worse. The Indian policy makers and industry advisors seem to see great merit in integrated steel plants and hence integrated facilities seem to have become the fashionable thing to do without carefully considering that integration would often mean a great aggregating capability in the management to be able to oversee distinct operations and yet synergize them harmoniously. Integration of facilities often means the unnecessary carrying of excess capacities and foregoing the flexibility of operations of stand-alone plants; in a time of overcapacity this could be debilitating on debts. No wonder then that in most of the above cases, the losses outstrip the invested money.

The other reason for bad loans in steel plants as cited above has been their desire to acquire assets such as land for mineral properties as well as factory sites. The huge land assets, which served as attractive collateral for the lending banks, were often acquired with enthusiasm precisely because they would increase the loan worthiness of the steel companies. Unfortunately in times of a general overcapacity across the world in steel production, current incomes tend to be lower than the assets sunk. Thomas Piketty argues in his book, *Capital*, that once the assets outstrip the current incomes by a ratio of 4:1 or even 3:1, current business operations tend to dampen off and get extinguished. The overextension of assets is also illustrated in the fact that both Bhushan Steel and Essar Steel sell older assets and acquire newer ones and in this manner shift investments from assets which are giving returns to assets which are new and yet to give returns. This strange manner of restructuring investments increase the burden of debt.

Appendix I

Table 10A.1 Industry sectorwise outstanding loans due to banks

No. 16: Industrywise deployment of gross bank credit (Rs Billion)						
Industry	Outstanding as on				Growth (%)	
	Mar. 20, 2015	2015	2016		Financial year so far	Y-o-Y
		Feb. 20	Jan. 22	Feb. 19	2015–16	2016
	1	2	3	4	5	6
1 Industry	26,576	26,058	27,244	27,455	3.3	5.4
1.1 Mining and quarrying (incl. coal)	360	364	387	392	9.0	7.7
1.2 Food processing	1,715	1,636	1,525	1,534	−10.6	−6.2
1.2.1 Sugar	414	375	365	380	−8.3	1.3
1.2.2 Edible oils and vanaspati	211	200	193	196	−7.2	−2.3
1.2.3 Tea	32	32	36	36	12.4	12.1
1.2.4 Others	1,058	1,029	931	923	−12.8	−10.3
1.3 Beverage and tobacco	186	185	178	185	−0.7	0.2
1.4 Textiles	2,019	1,998	2,027	2,044	1.2	2.3
1.4.1 Cotton textiles	1,000	990	1,017	1,029	2.9	3.9
1.4.2 Jute textiles	22	22	22	22	−2.3	−2.1
1.4.3 Man-made textiles	204	203	208	209	2.6	3.1
1.4.4 Other textiles	793	783	780	784	−1.1	0.2
1.5 Leather and leather products	102	101	103	104	1.5	3.4
1.6 Wood and wood products	98	97	96	96	−2.0	−0.9

No. 16: Industrywise deployment of gross bank credit (Rs Billion)

Industry	Outstanding as on				Growth (%)	
	Mar. 20, 2015	2015	2016		Financial year so far	Y-o-Y
		Feb. 20	Jan. 22	Feb. 19	2015–16	2016
	1	2	3	4	5	6
1.7 Paper and paper products	341	339	362	358	5.2	5.7
1.8 Petroleum, coal products and uclear fuels	561	539	477	475	−15.3	−11.8
1.9 Chemicals and chemical products	1,545	1,504	1,562	1,589	2.9	5.7
1.9.1 Fertilizer	254	243	229	256	0.7	5.1
1.9.2 Drugs and pharmaceuticals	493	481	513	518	5.1	7.7
1.9.3 Petro chemicals	331	334	362	354	7.0	5.9
1.9.4 Others	467	446	458	462	−1.2	3.5
1.10 Rubber, plastic and their products	378	375	363	368	−2.6	−1.8
1.11 Glass and glassware	88	89	89	88	0.1	−0.8
1.12 Cement and cement products	560	559	538	537	−4.2	−4.0
1.13 Basic metal and metal product	3,854	3,760	4,099	4,145	7.6	10.2
1.13.1 Iron and steel	2,834	2,753	3,037	3,090	9.0	12.3
1.13.2 Other metal and metal product	1,020	1,007	1,062	1,055	3.5	4.8
1.14 All engineering	1,540	1,521	1,526	1,539	−0.1	1.1
1.14.1 Electronics	368	363	379	382	3.8	5.2
1.14.2 Others	1,172	1,158	1,147	1,157	−1.3	−0.1
1.15 Vehicles, vehicle parts and transport equipment	682	667	679	678	−0.5	1.7
1.16 Gems and jewellery	718	714	718	728	1.3	1.9

(continued)

Table 10A.1 Continued

No. 16: Industrywise deployment of gross bank credit (Rs Billion)						
Industry	Outstanding as on				Growth (%)	
	Mar. 20, 2015	2015	2016		Financial year so far	Y-o-Y
		Feb. 20	Jan. 22	Feb. 19	2015–16	2016
	1	2	3	4	5	6
1.17 Construction	743	746	739	746	0.4	0.0
1.18 Infrastructure	9,245	9,115	9,883	9,944	7.6	9.1
1.18.1 Power	5,576	5,514	5,992	6,045	8.4	9.6
1.18.2 Telecommunications	919	858	937	939	2.1	9.4
1.18.3 Roads	1,687	1,675	1,789	1,794	6.4	7.1
1.18.4 Other infrastructure	1,064	1,068	1,165	1,166	9.6	9.3
1.19 Other industries	1,839	1,751	1,892	1,904	3.5	8.8

Note: Data are provisional and relate to select banks which cover 95 per cent of total non-food credit extended by all scheduled commercial banks (excludes ING Vysya which has been merged with Kotak Mahindra since April 2015).
Export credit under priority sector relates to foreign banks only.
Micro and small under item 2.1 includes credit to micro and small industries in manufacturing sector.
Micro and small enterprises under item 5.2 includes credit to micro and small enterprises in manufacturing as well as services sector.
Priority Sector is as per old definition and does not conform to FIDD Circular FIDD.CO.Plan. BC.54/04.09.01/2014-15 dated April 23, 2015.
Source: RBI Bulletin, April 2016.

Notes

1 www.business-standard.com/article/finance/bank-loan-to-steel-sector-grew-21-over-past-5-years-115081001434_1.html
2 www.bloomberg.com/news/articles/2016-03-14/day-of-reckoning-coming-for-india-s-pigs-with-lipstick-lenders
3 http://timesofindia.indiatimes.com/business/india-business/Steel-loans-worth-50k-cr-may-turn-bad-in-few-months/articleshow/51545264.cms
4 http://articles.economictimes.indiatimes.com/2015-06-26/news/63862357_1_steel-industry-steel-sector-banking-stability-indicator
5 www.business-standard.com/article/companies/uttam-galva-acquires-lloyds-steel-to-invest-rs-380-cr-more-112111800042_1.html
6 Ibid.
7 "Uttam Galva Steels on the Block", Businessline, Hindu, 1 July 2016, p. 1.
8 www.business-standard.com/article/companies/shree-uttam-steel-power-to-set-up-rs-11-156-cr-mega-project-in-mah-114022701091_1.html
9 http://economictimes.indiatimes.com/industry/indl-goods/svs/metals-mining/essar-steel-bags-iron-ore-mine-in-odisha/articleshow/51248118.cms
10 www.thehindu.com/business/Industry/the-biggestever-fire-sale-of-indian-corporate-assets-has-begun-to-tide-over-bad-loans-crisis/article8573163.ece

11 http://economictimes.indiatimes.com/industry/indl-goods/svs/metals-mining/essar-steel-bags-iron-ore-mine-in-odisha/articleshow/51248118.cms
12 Op. cit. 9
13 www.electrosteel.com/group-companies/lanco.aspx
14 http://timesofindia.indiatimes.com/business/india-business/Steel-loans-worth-50k-cr-may-turn-bad-in-few-months/articleshow/51545264.cms
15 www.financialexpress.com/industry/visa- steel-to-turn-npa-in-banks-books/226108/

11 Technologies for making steel

For the steel industry in India, the policy makers and especially, the Ministry of Steel have always believed and followed the model of Joseph Schumpeter (1949) of capitalist development, in the sense that innovations were the foundations upon which profits were created and scale of production expanded.[1] This is why, in times of demand and supply gaps, especially, whenever demand has outstripped supply, the Ministry of Steel brought about a sense of urgency in the industry to innovate. There are two major institutions for research and development, both in the public sector: the Research and Development Centre for Iron and Steel, or RDCIS, in Ranchi, and Biju Pattanaik National Institute for Steel, or BPNIS, in Puri. Technologies have principally been improvements in electric steelmaking, and include innovations in refractories and steel refining, innovations in raw materials such as directly reduced iron ore and greater levels of plant expansions through larger machinery. Interestingly, it is the last mentioned that has the least potential for innovation and has largely braced the large steel plants in the integrated sector. Fortunately, for India, since its industry was controlled by industrial licenses for a long time, and it was not before the middle of the 1970s when demand for steel jumped suddenly and capacities were still to come forth, innovations in terms of new processes and new kinds of raw materials were, namely, in the form of the electric arc furnaces.

Steel technologies from 1907 to 1967

The thrust of innovations all through the above period was to be able to indigenize steelmaking technology as a part of the great swadeshi, or do-it-yourself mission of the Independence movement of India. After Independence, technologies were imported from UK, Germany and the USSR to set up integrated steel plants. Steel plants were retrofitted, indigenized and adapted to local conditions, especially the coke ovens. It was not really until the 1980s, when all steel plants were expanded and modernized that indiginous technologies in steelmaking were introduced. These were the times of import substitution, since India was importing high-quality flat steel from Belgium and Japan. A part of expansion was to integrate more and more downstream products, such as cold rolling and galvanizing.

Steel technologies of the 1980s and the 1990s

Steel technologies in India can be divided into two broad segments: one for the large integrated steel plants, and the other for the smaller secondary steel mills. The developments in the above have followed very different trajectories. Interestingly, most episodes in technological progress took place during the 1980s and the 1990s in response to the growth in the steel markets in India, and not really due to the economic liberalization. This means that technologically India's best period was during the days of industrial controls and not after its dismantling. All through the 1980s and the 1990s, we observe that steel production capacities had to struggle to meet a galloping demand for steel. While extensive modernization programmes were undertaken in the public sector steel plants and in Tata Steel, then still known as TISCO, it was the secondary steel sector that really should get the credit for bringing the most innovations on board; its innovations were home grown.

The 1980s was the period of growth for electric arc furnaces in India; scrap was allowed to be imported. Though the electric arc furnace was designed for producing high carbon and other alloy steel for tool applications, the Indians reoriented it to be able to produce mild steel. The crux of such an innovation was to perfect the ladle refining of steel, vacuum degassing and of course, technologies for scrap bundling and shredding. Not only were technologies retrofitted and redesigned, but a major difference between the way innovations were handled by the integrated steel plants and the secondary producers was that in the former, technologies were one off, but in the latter they were synergized and coordinated (and formed harmonious wholes). The aim of the electric furnace industry during this point of time was to be able to produce similar qualities and comparable grades of mild steel as the large integrated steel mills. Apropos to the electric arc furnaces, the rolling mills also revved up by improving their activities. Of course, many rolling mills increased their capacities; but, the major innovation in this period was the tandem mill, in which rolling could be done in one go, without stopping. No wonder, then, that the 1980s was the period of the rise of the electric arc furnaces.

The integrated steel plants continued to modernize, but such modernizations were, mainly, in the realm of expansion of steelmaking capacities, in continuous casting (by which steel rolling and casting episodes could be better integrated by not breaking the heat cycle), in the increase in the capacities and speed of the rolling activities and to an extent in the chemical engineering aspects of pickling and annealing. Technologies that could manage recovery of heat better, or improve the technical norms for raw materials, did not figure in the technology bouquet of the integrated steel plants. Since raw materials, were assured for these large mills, including TISCO (now Tata Steel), in the private sector, these mills did not have to undertake technologies to augment the quality of raw materials nor did they have to invest in refining in a manner in which the secondary steel sector had to.

In the 1990s, two major indigenous innovations shook at the very foundations of the Indian steel industry; and these were the coming of the sponge iron industry and induction furnaces. India invented neither of the above, but made incremental changes, so that today, it is the world's largest producer of sponge iron as well as of mild steel through induction furnaces; India produced 20 million tonnes of sponge iron and 50 million tonnes of mild steel through induction and electric steel furnaces. Nowhere in the world has directly reduced iron, which is sponge iron and the induction furnace, principally a contraption for the production of stainless steel, gold, copper and silver, been so extensively used for the production of mild steel! The scale was achieved through two means: for the sponge iron it was the use of the coal-based small sized rotary kilns, while for the induction furnaces, it was the post-melting refining that made large-scale production possible. A word of caution is needed here: the scale of the individual plants did not increase; what increased were the large number of players in the market, which added up to such huge quantities.

Also, the induction furnaces were designed in such a manner by which they could almost wholly use sponge iron, instead of scrap. Since India has rich deposits of iron ore, the quality of steel was assured, because the quality of iron ore was assured. Induction furnaces were assured of endless supplies of raw materials, and sponge iron meant that steel could now be produced without the help of coking coal, an input for which India has to principally depend on imports. With innovations such as hot charging and continuous casting, the induction furnace became as good as a steel melting shop. Induction furnaces were cheaper than the arc furnaces, and India emerged not only as a major steel producer, but also was very cost competitive, because all through the 1990s, it was a net exporter of steel, especially, to the Asian region, Middle East and Africa, the latter two being India's conventional destination for exports.

Post-liberalization technologies: changing pattern of steel use

Technologies in the post-liberalization 1990s, precisely the decade when innovations were taking place in the induction furnaces and sponge iron sector, included integrated steel plants entering the age of reheating furnaces, in which rolling becomes more productive; reheating helps to integrate the casting and the rolling activities of the steel plants, especially when integrated mills want to diversify into downstream products. Clearly, technology was tied to market outreach. The electric arc furnaces were quieter by now, focusing on refractories and management of slag generation, both to achieve better energy economics. Between 1994 and 2008, steel production really increased, propelling India from the eight largest steel producer in the world to the third position. But, times were changing, and rising imports, despite rising production, constituted the greatest worry; India had to prepare itself for manufacturing world class steel, especially for the manufacturing units for consumer durables that companies from Japan and Korea had set up in India. By 2010, cheap steel from China flooded the market, as well. The investments in infrastructure projects (by which flyovers, metro rails, high rise apartment buildings, ports and airports are supposed to be built) purports to change the pattern of steel use in them; grades of steel which perhaps the induction furnaces would make and roll out through smaller rolling mills may no longer serve the cause of the new steel applications. The new age steel may have to be stronger and sterner and of a good quality; the change in the quality of steel has been the hardest blow on the future of indigenous steel in India. *To the best of my mind, it is more the pattern of steel consumption rather than cheap imports that has hurt the Indian steel industry the most.*

Technologies in the new millennium took metallurgy more seriously, because the quality of steel can only be improved through a fundamental change in the way steel is produced in the furnaces. Nippon Steel and Kobe Steel helped the large integrated sector, like Tata Steel, Bhushan Steel, JSW and SAIL, to upgrade coke-making and iron-making technologies. One of the most remarkable changes was the use of iron ore fines, DRI and pellets for the blast furnaces in SAIL plants. The introduction of the new age coke oven into the Indian steel industry's oxygen furnaces by Kobe Steel was a major step in both heat recovery as well as in the quality of coke obtained, which had enormous prospects for the quality of hot metal. In the induction furnace sector, hot charging of sponge iron and special efforts at slag management, were supposed to bring about the corresponding benefits of energy optimization and the control of properties of molten steel. However, besides the efforts at the control of quality, the integrated steel mills are also experimenting with possibilities of new kinds of raw materials, especially the pulverized coal injections and also the use of iron ore fines in blast furnaces.

There is a distinct effort at *integrating the rolling and the casting operations*, especially because by 2000 continuous casting came to stay in India, though the proportion of steel continuously cast is still at about 80%; the rest of the world is close to 100%.[2] The induction furnace sector, too, has experimented successfully with the continuous casting of thin sections. Continuous casting is an energy saver and provides more consistent steel quality.

The tendency in the present world is to use *qualities of raw materials hitherto considered as "unusable"* by the steel industry, namely non-coking coal and iron ore fines. Technologies, like Corex, Finex, Fasmelt, Hismelt and the various technologies of direct reduction of iron ore, have not only paved the way for the use of iron ore fines, but also, shown us the path to be independent of coking coal. Add to this the latest developments in iron ore beneficiation, and the world seems all set to use iron ore with lower ferrous content; and in this way, expand the supplies of the mineral to unprecedented bounties.

The principal concern of the steel industry of the world at this moment is the *management of pollution* emanating out of the steel industry. Steel manufacturing is one of the most polluting industries, emitting twice as much carbon as the tonnage of its final product; the present day technological innovations are geared towards the management of emissions and heat recovery, prevention and treatment of effluents (and of course management in the quality of raw materials) in order to address the problem of pollution at the core. These three classes of technology have the possibility of improving the energy economics of steel mills, and give us cleaner environments. Companies, like Hatch Beddows and Danieli Corus, now have greater revenues from the management of the environment; environment management is becoming a major business now. Please see Figure 11.1.

In earlier chapters, we spoke about the conflict over market space between the integrated steel mills and the electric furnaces; there may well be a technology

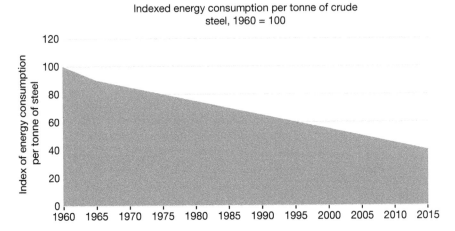

Figure 11.1 Decline in energy consumption for crude steel production

Source: www.worldsteel.org/publications/fact-sheets/content/02/text_files/file0/document/fact_
energy_2016.pdf

angle to that, as well. Indian iron ore is high in phosphorous, which is a welcome property of steel when steel is flat; in long products, phosphorous creates intra-molecular gaps that cause steel high in phosphorous to become brittle. Indian iron ore favours the flat steel producers, which, unfortunately, have to be the bigger plants (because casting flats requires larger facilities, thus automatically pushing the smaller plants into a corner). *The reduction of phosphorous* is crucial to the secondary sector, especially in view of the Quality Control Order, in which grades are closely specified.

Global division of technology

Globally, there seems to be division of the world, in terms of developments in technology. Japan has chosen to specialize in coal and coke-making technologies, having already achieved its limits in product development; China is now into iron ore beneficiation and the management of phosphorous in iron ore (because of the gargantuan stocks of Indian ore lying in the country). Since phosphorous is good for flat steels but fragile for long products, Chinese steelmakers have introduced boron into long steel (in order to compensate for the brittleness that the presence of phosphorous brings about and thus, created a new product, as well as a new way of thinking through the solution of brittleness of steel). European steelmakers are principally concerned with pollution control technologies, while German companies such as SMS Group, namely SMS Seimag AG and SMS Demag, and others, manufacture machinery and equipment geared towards the integration of plant processes and the optimal management of heat.

Low performance of Indian steel plants in technological parameters against international benchmarks: a matter of low skill?

Presented in Table 11.1 is a comparison between the Indian steel plants and the international benchmarked particulars of productivity. It shows, clearly, that the performance of the Indian steel plants are below those of the best in the world. The table shows that irrespective of the blast furnace or the electric furnace routes, the performance of the Indian steel mills is below those of international benchmarks; this is despite the fact that India has perhaps the finest quality of iron ore and

Table 11.1 Comparative performance across various technology parameters of Indian steel plants and international benchmarks as of February 2013

Particulars	Indian actuals	International benchmark
Sinter plant productivity, t/hr/m2	1.2-1.5	1.8
Blast furnace productivity, t/d/m3	1.5-2.5	2.5-3.5
Blast furnace coke rate, kg/thm	400-550	300-400
PCI in blast furnace, kg/thm	50-150	150-250
Agglomerates in blast furnace, % of weight of feed	60-80	80-90
Blast furnace slag volume, kg/thm	300-400	200-300
Blast furnace campaign life	8-12 years	12-15 years
Net coal consumption (ash is 25%), t/tof DRI	0.8-1.2	0.75-0.85
Feed of gas based DRI plants, ore: pellets	60:40	30:70
BOF no. of heats per converter annually	5000-9000	8000-12000

(continued)

Table 11.1 Continued

Particulars	Indian actuals	International benchmark
BOF life of lining in number of heats	2000-10000	8000-15000
Tap to tap time in BOF, min	45-60	30-45
EAF furnace size, tonnes	50-150	100-250
Tap to tap time in EAF, min	75-100	50-70
Power consumption in EAF, kwh/tonne	400-600	150-350
EAF specific productivity, t/hr/MVA	0.5 -0.7	0.8-1.5
Slag volume BOF/EAF, kgs/tcs	150-200	50-100
Sulphur, ppm	10-100	5-100
Phosphorous	50-200	10-150
Oxygen	10-50	5-40
Nitrogen	30-60	10-40
Continuous casting speed, m/min		
Slab	1.0-1.9	1.5-2.5
Billet	3-3.5	3.5-4.5
Bloom	0.5-0.9	0.6-1
Hot strip mill utilization, %	80	90
Yield, %	97.5	98.5
Cold rolling mill utilization, %	65	95
Yield, %	94.5	95
Yield of finished steel from liquid steel	85 to 90	88 to 92

Table 11.1 Continued

Particulars	Indian actuals	International benchmark
Specific energy consumption, Gcal/tcs	5.5-7	4.5-5.5
BF-BOF process	1500-2000	1200-1800
EAF process	600-900	150-350
Specific dust emission, kg/tcs	0.85-1.15	0.5-0.75
Solid waste utilization, %	85-90	90-95
Water pollutant discharge, kg/tcs	0.07-0.125	zero

Source: N.M. Rao. Indian Steel Industry - Challenges and Tasks Ahead. ISR. February 2013. Kolkata.

good quality non-coking coal, and because coking coal is largely imported, there can be no issues on the quality of raw materials. Additionally, the technologies used by the large integrated steel plants are imported (and therefore as good as anywhere in the world). Unfortunately, there has never been a systematic study on the low levels of performance of the Indian steel plants.

Technology mission of the Ministry of Steel

The technology mission under the aegis of the Ministry of Steel,[3] known as the R&D mission, operates around three coordinates. First is the beneficiation and upgrade of raw materials, which is in the short term. Secondly, there is a thrust on product development and insistence on new products; this is the medium term. In the long term, plans are afloat to utilize wasteful emissions, like use of slag in steelmaking, treatment of effluents and so on. The core of steel technology across the world, namely the better management of heat and the control of emissions, do not appear to constitute the crux of the technology mission of the Ministry of Steel. However, in a collaborative effort with the Global Environment Facility, or GEF, the UNDP has helped smaller rolling mills in India to make changes towards the control of pollution that has automatically improved their technical parameters and reduced costs.

India has made some remarkable progress in its small sponge iron plants, adapting the rotary kiln, using coal as the main source of energy and as the carbon reductant. India has made good progress in cold processing and galvanizing, since it is only the galvanizing sheet producing segment in India (which is globally competitive). India has the ability to produce extra thin sheets, unparalleled anywhere in the world. These innovations have been put together by small producers and not by the large integrated steel plants; small producers have always been looked down upon in the hallowed portals of the Ministry, and discounted in any kind of media reportage. Yet, it is this segment that has really held the competitiveness of the Indian steel industry together. One needs to acknowledge the discounted people as contributors to the technology growth of the steel sector. For the Ministry, it has only been the white-collared employees in the organized work world of the large units who have counted, and unfortunately, this social class of steel workers have not been able to contribute to the development of steelmaking technology in India.

A short note on skills

It is easy to observe that the technology innovations of the secondary steel sector have been more organic, of the in-house and on the floor type, rather than something imposed from above (as a management or a ministerial decision). The latter kind has happened in integrated steel plants, which have gone more for adoption of technology, rather than organically emerging into states of higher technology. In the previous chapter on bad loans, we observed that while the defaulting companies have adopted technology, they have been unable to integrate them into an organically united single production entity. The skill that India needs in its steel industry at the moment is the ability to integrate operations. The Iron and Steel Sector Skills Council, set up under the suggestions of the National Skills Mission, once again, uses different kinds of skills needed in the steel industry discreetly (rather than making efforts at integrating them). Steelmaking is an interdisciplinary subject that requires metallurgy, chemistry, thermodynamics, chemical engineering, electrical and mechanical engineering, fluid mechanics, automation and mathematical modelling; it is important that the skill of integration be developed among the steel professionals. There is also a need to combine strategic marketing skills with skills of production and operations management and steelmaking technological knowledge.

Swings in innovations: Chinese incursions

The upward swing of the Indian steel industry took place with innovations in the small-scale secondary sector of electric furnaces. The innovations were, mainly, in the design of furnaces, use of post-melting refining and manipulation of processes to use more and more locally available raw materials (in the form of directly reduced iron). Today, the cycle of innovations has flattened out and perhaps, were we to abide by Schumpeter's thesis on innovations; this is the cause of the weaknesses of the Indian industry.

It is possible to view the Chinese incursions in terms of innovations as well; China has evolved in the manufacture of steel in leaps and bounds, although it has yet to be able to master electrical steelmaking. However, its innovations in the blast furnace that can now digest a variety of raw materials, especially pellets from beneficiated ore, and its rolling mills which can continuously roll hot steel, have created near havoc across the world. In the face of China, India has two possibilities of holding out: its fantastic ability to produce through the induction furnace, and its ability to produce the world's thinnest gauge of galvanized steel; these are the two products in which India is unbeatable.

Conclusion

The chapter started with the thesis of Joseph Schumpeter, that innovations are critical to the boom and bust period of steel, and we observe that periods of technological growth have, indeed, corresponded with the growth in the steel industry. The present stagnation in the industry can perhaps, only be lifted with the right kind of innovation in steel production; and we are grappling with the direction and the source from which that innovation will emerge. The secondary steel sector has been the engine of innovations in India; and hence, the engine of growth, while the large integrated steel plants have mainly adopted and adapted to already standardized technology developed elsewhere in the world; this has been the reason why steel production, led by the large integrated steel plants, ends up in stagnation, all too soon in India. As a quick recapitulation from the chapter on bad loans, it is clear that technological incompetence for integrating the various technologies was a major reason for the failure of projects.

Notes

1 Joseph Schumpeter's thesis that economic booms are caused by cycles of innovations and not cycles of banks is cited in www.dailyreckoning.com.au/business-cycle-joseph-schumpeter/2008/10/02/.
2 Steel Statistical Yearbook, 2015. IISI, Brussels.
3 http://steel.gov.in/scheme%20for%20promotion%20of%20research%20&%20development%20in%20indian%20iron%20&%20steel%20industry.htm

12 The cost of steel

Whether steel will be profitable to manufacture will depend on its price and costs. The costs will depend on technology used, and the efficiency with which it is used in converting raw materials to finished products; the lower the costs are, the higher is the margin of the firm and consequently, the higher is the enthusiasm to expand and grow in scale. The cost of making steel, like every kind of business, has been estimated as a set of fixed and variable costs, the fixed costs being those attributed to the plant and machinery, sometimes a fixed proportion of total cost, such as depreciation, salaries and wages of permanent labour force, while the variable costs are those attributed to raw materials, electricity, fuel, utilities, transport and so on. Plants with new state of the art technology can produce steel more economically, but in order to be able to sell steel really cheap, the costs of plant and machinery must be absorbed (in the sense that debts against the investments must be all paid off). Older plants may carry less fixed costs because their capital costs, or CAPEX, are all paid off, dues cleared and debts settled, but these plants may use older technology and may not always produce steel cheap. Fixed costs are paradoxical; those plants that have large fixed costs are often the new investments that have the potential to produce low-cost steel, while those with lower fixed costs because the CAPEX is all covered, are also ones with older technologies. In times of growing technologies, fixed costs are really not a problem, and plants can expand with enough price margin to initiate new technologies; in times of standardized technologies, expansions in capacities may mean only the fattening up of fixed costs. It is not advisable to expand steel-making capacities until, and unless, there is a distinct step up in technologies, as well.

The variable costs mainly constitute raw materials and power and fuel. Raw materials are minerals, like iron ore, coal, various alloying minerals (like manganese and chromium, limestone and dolomite) and other coating elements, like zinc. The prices of raw materials constitute anywhere between 40% and 60% of the cost of producing steel. Raw material prices are determined by demand and supply, but also, in the long term, by proportion of current output to reserves; interestingly, the lower the ratio of production to reserves is, the higher the price is. Miners operate with interesting psychologies; they are eager to sell when resources in their mines are nearing their end; prices go down, as resources near exhaustion. Hence, the discovery of new deposits may assure us of plenty, but these also tend to raise the resource prices. Theories of rent by David Ricardo may be invoked here, to say that the new mines need higher investments, as compared to the reserves, which are already in the process of mining, and hence, price rises to cover the costs of investing in the new mines. In fact, a noise emanates from the steel industry in India, which is to let us exhaust our mineral reserves as fast as we can, because exhaustion is a way of tendering them cheap.

Power and fuel constitute yet another component of variable costs, and power prices often depend upon demand and supply, but also, on the cost of fuel. For countries that import fuels, especially fossil fuels, the costs will depend on the basket of commodities that they export to earn the revenues, in order to buy fuel. Clearly, then, fuel costs depends upon the export competitiveness of fuel-importing countries; expectedly, then, the Indian steelmakers incessantly complain about fuel costs being higher than anywhere else in the world, without realizing that manufacturing needs to be competitive first, and, only then can fuel costs for a fuel-importing country, like that of India, come down.

Is India really a low-cost steelmaker?

In the 1990s, India prided itself as a low-cost steelmaker in the world; however, in present times, it is in fact, a country with relatively higher costs of production (as we see from the data from SAIL and Tata Steel) in comparison to some of the world's largest and best operated steel plants. A part of the reason for high costs is possibly the large capital outlays, which have been recently made by way of capacity expansions in the Indian mills. Contrary to claims by the Indian steelmakers that interest costs are very high in India, Table 12.1 shows that this is not the case. But strangely, despite India being a country of low wages, labour costs are relatively higher in the Indian plants, and so are the material costs, despite Indian plants, as mentioned above, having captive iron ore reserves.

Table 12.1 Fixed and variable costs of select steel mills across the world

2010	Units	US Steel Corporation	NUCOR Steel	Nippon Steel	Posco	Tata Steel	SAIL	Bao Steel
Fixed costs to total costs	%	14.1	11.9	17.9	18.5	24.3	25.4	12.7
Steel sector labour cost per tonne of production	USD	141.3	62.6	51.4	42.5	81.3	127.4	8.7
Material and other costs per tonne of production	USD	616.4	517.4	715.6	603.2	508.8	711.8	485.4

(*continued*)

Table 12.1 Continued

2010	Units	US Steel Corporation	NUCOR Steel	Nippon Steel	Posco	Tata Steel	SAIL	Bao Steel
Steel sector interest cost per tonne of production	USD	12.3	7	6.4	8.2	7.5	2.8	8.4
Steel sector depreciation cost per tonne	USD	29.6	22.4	65.1	58.2	23.5	55.7	44.4
Steel sector material costs per tonne of production	USD	574.5	488	644.1	536.8	478.6	477.8	653.3
Steel sector pre-tax income per tonne of production	USD	−17	47	23.1	132.2	303.7	112.2	75.1
Steel sector capital outlay per tonne of capacity	USD	23.4	7.7	62.1	107	120.7	140.3	37.5
Steel sector capital outlay per tonne produced	USD	30.4	11.2	61.5	109	123.3	168.9	39.2

Source: World Steel Dynamics, Financial Dynamics.

Chinese versus non-Chinese mills

World Steel Dynamics has compiled data to work out the averages of the Chinese and the non-Chinese steel plants in the world (Table 12.2). It has been observed that the revenues, revenue margins and gross margins of the Chinese mills are lower than those of the non-Chinese mills. The expenses of the Chinese mills are lower than those of the non-Chinese mills, material costs being substantially lower than the non-Chinese mills. China has its own metallurgical coal, and hence, coke, but it has purchased almost half of its iron ore from all over the world (and driven the prices of iron ore to four times its base prices in 2004). Interest costs are only marginally lower for China, and so are depreciation and labour costs. But revenues of the Chinese mills are also lower; China sells very cheap. The Chinese are willing to work at much lower margins and profitability than the rest of the firms. The revenues for the non-Chinese mills are USD $109 against $46 for the Chinese mills; yet, the non-Chinese mills seem to be complaining of low profits, while the Chinese mills, even at a fraction of the profits of the non-Chinese mills, prepare to expand production and overrun the world with a crusader's zeal.

Table 12.2 Costs in USD per tonne shipped for non-Chinese and Chinese mills

| Per tonne shipped in USD | In USD per tonne shipped in 2013 | | |
	Non-Chinese	Chinese mills	Differences between the non-Chinese and Chinese mills
Labour	96	56	40
Material	804	682	122
Interest	17	13	4
Depreciation	53	41	12
Total expenses	971	792	179
Capital outlays	83	92	−9
Total assets	1148	956	193
EBDITDA	91	66	26
Revenue from sales	1060	855	205
Other income	20	0	20
Total revenue	1080	855	225
Revenue minus expenses	109	63	46

Source: Ibid.

Table 12.3 Variable cost of production of steel in Rs/tonne

Plants	2007–08	2008–09	2009–10	2010–11	2011–12
SAIL	14950	20385	19717	20635	24787
Tata Steel	18311	23445	21136	20374	26042
RINL	21699	22286	23676	25867	32264
JSWL	24554	33342	25327	28108	35589
JSPL	23575	31621	23539	24834	31147
JSW Ispat	23238	29930	28521	31351	38759
Essar Steel	23265	26629			

Source: N.M. Rao. *Iron and Steel Review*. Kolkata. February 2013.

Variable costs of Indian integrated steel firms

In industries such as steel, which are both large scale and high technology, technological innovations constantly replace machines and there is continual investment
in what becomes accounted for as fixed costs. Manufacturers, especially of high-
end products, tend to watch the averages rather than the marginal costs, and here,
they look to covering their average variable costs. In February 2013, N.M. Rao
calculated the costs of making steel of the large integrated steel plants (Table 12.3).[1]

Table 12.4 Average selling price of steel in Rs/tonne

Plants	2007–08	2008–09	2009–10	2010–11	2011–12
SAIL	34000	40000	34000	38000	42000
Tata Steel	35000	41000	35000	37500	43000
RINL	31000	36000	35000	35000	41000
JSWL	35000	41000	35000	39000	41000
JSPL	30000	3000	37000	34000	41000
JSW Ispat	32000	42000	33000	38000	41000

Source: Ibid.

Table 12.5 Average margins to cover fixed costs of steel companies in Rs/tonne

Plants	2007–08	2008–09	2009–10	2010–11	2011–12
SAIL	19050	19615	14283	17365	17213
Tata Steel	16689	17555	13864	17126	16958
RINL	9301	13714	11324	9133	8736
JSWL	10446	7658	9673	10892	5411
JSPL	6425	−28621	13461	9166	9853
JSW Ispat	8762	12070	4479	6649	2241

Source: Compiled from Tables 12.1, 12.2, 12.3 and 12.4.

The lower variable costs of SAIL and Tata Steel are due to the captive source of raw materials. We subtract the variable costs in Table 12.3 from the average selling price in Table 12.4 to obtain Table 12.5.

It is very clear from Table 12.5 that SAIL and Tata Steel have wider margins to cover fixed costs because they have captive mines, and thus, have access to a cheap and in-house source of raw materials. Those plants that do not have captive sources of raw materials have lower margins, as they have to procure raw materials or bid for mining properties. The above-mentioned plants are, thus, best poised to pursue technological innovations, and in times to come, these are the firms that ideally, should emerge as technology leaders of the Indian steel industry.

Cost structure of firms across industry segments in India

Now that we have fairly agreed that the large integrated steel mills are not cost competitive to stand with the best firms across the world, we may as well consider how the large cap plants perform, in terms of costs, as compared to the small and medium steelmakers and to the stand-alone steel processors, in India. Presented in Table 12.6 are the aggregates from the annual results of the companies published by www.moneycontrol.com.[2]

Table 12.6 Performance indicators as percentage of net sales for the listed steel companies in India

	Net profit	PBDIT	Inventory	Raw materials	Power and fuels	Employment cost
Large cap	8.01	20.29	25.72	46.38	8.69	11.46
Medium and small	−4.52	16.58	36.00	63.95	8.94	3.75
Rolling mills	−2.26	7.94	15.38	73.42	7.44	3.43
Hot rolled/ cold rolled	−10.00	18.46	61.44	62.03	10.78	2.59
GP/GC sheets	1.17	8.40	17.39	83.26	1.62	2.10
Total	4.89	18.72	28.20	51.92	8.48	9.38

Source: Author's compilation from www.moneycontrol.com.

Raw material costs as percentages of net sales are the lowest for the large cap integrated plants and the highest for the GP/GC sheets because, for the latter, raw materials are the finished products of the hot rolled/cold rolled mills. In fact, apart from the large cap companies, no other segment uses minerals as the raw materials. Inventory costs are the highest for the hot rolled/cold rolled companies; it is possible to link this to the slight underproduction of coils by the integrated steel mills, necessitating large-scale imports. Inventories are held due to uncertainty of domestic availability, and the import restrictions, by way of safeguards and Minimum Import Prices, of these products. Power and fuel are not unusually high, and employment costs appear to be just about the global average for the large caps (and abysmally low for the rest of the industry segments).

The variable costs of the Indian steel plants have been obtained from the published accounts of the companies listed in the National Stock Exchange and indicated under the various categories (such as Large Caps, Small and Medium Steel Producers and so on). Since the production figures in tonnage have not been provided for these plants, costs have been worked out as percentage of net sales. The large steel mills seem to be the best positioned in terms of variable costs as a percentage of their net sales, and are thus, ready to expand. The rolling mills and the galvanized plants are most vulnerable, and any slight increase in the costs of their raw materials, power, fuel and wages may retard their growth. No wonder then, that the large integrated plants also have the best profits and the rest of the segments have the poorest.

Conclusions

Cost of production can also be decoded in terms of episodes in the life of an industry; higher fixed costs may mean higher investments into higher levels of technology, while lower fixed costs may also mean the end of the road for a firm in its growth. Investments into fixed assets, ideally, should bring about higher levels of technology that will help reduce the variable costs; were plants to only expand capacities without any upgrade of technologies, they would fall into the burden of overheads (without any kinds of gains for steel production). Variable costs, which consist of raw materials and fuel, are dependent on the state of the mining industry; newer mines raise the price of minerals while old mines tend to lower them. Fuel prices are tied up to the overall export competitiveness of economies like India, which are net importers of fuel. Large cap companies do better, in terms of lower costs, because they use minerals as raw materials, while the stand-alone and fragmented plants do worse because they use mill products as their raw materials. Among the large caps, SAIL and Tata Steel do better than JSW because they have captive mines, while JSW has to purchase minerals from the market. India is not a low-cost steel producer, and its main producers, who have the lowest cost of production within the country, do not fare well competitively in the world; this means that the steel industry of India is a high-cost industry, and expanding will mean a waste of resources. China sells cheap, not because its costs are the lowest, but its prices are low because the Chinese companies are willing to work for lower profits.

Appendix I: consolidated accounts of steel plants

Table 12A.1 Costs and profits of steel producers

	Large integrated	Small and medium steel producers	Rolling mills	HR/CR	GP/GC
Net profit/net sales %	8.01	−4.2	−4.95	−9.82	1.32
PBDIT/net sales %	20.29	15.77	8.61	18.13	8.52
Inventory turnover ratio	3.89	2.92	5.84	1.63	5.72
Raw materials/ net sales %	46.38	65.22	75.31	62.71	83.01
Power and fuels/ net sales %	8.69	8.94	6.96	10.78	1.64
Labour costs/net sales %	11.46	3.68	3.43	2.54	2.1
Total variable cost/net sales %	66.53	77.84	85.7	76.03	86.75
Investments/ total assets %	27.25	1.95	10.6	1.46	15.35

Source: www.moneycontrol.com and own calculations.

Appendix II: annual reports of various steel companies

Table 12A.2a Costs and profits of large cap steel companies

	Net sales	Net profit	PBDIT	Inventory	Raw materials	Power and fuels	Employment cost	Investments	Total assets
					Large cap steel companies				
Tata Steel	46087.32	6439.12	12482.43	8042	13956.45	2704.2	4601.92	53164.32	92607.12
JSW	45710.78	2166.48	8942.11	8584.74	28254.34	3475.67	946.88	4197.28	69749.32
SAIL	41785	2092.68	5674.65	17736.37	19749.44	5423.53	9763.33	909.07	51485.83
Total	133583.1	10698.28	27099.19	34363.11	61960.23	11603.4	15312.13	58270.67	213842.3

Source: www.moneycontrol.com

Table 12A.2b Costs and profits of medium and small companies

Small and medium cap steel mills

	Net sales	Net profit	PBDIT	Inventory	Raw materials	Power and fuels	Employment cost	Investments	Total assets
					Rs crores				
Jindal Stainless	6010.94	223.08	1529.99	1720.57	4445.23	637.48	115.63	103.43	10596.4
Usha Martin	3746.05	−292.41	546.22	1316.76	1522.17	381.23	239.88	167.74	4481.67
Mukand	2819.65	1.58	343.18	1423.58	1690.45	193.84	159.01	251	4219.14
Kamdhenu Ispat	967.99	8.03	30.31	64.86	821.87		24.31	3.42	192.41
Adhunik Industries	411.23	10.77	37.38	121.87	346.44	15.42	1.86	0.04	198.79
Rathi Bars	236.51	0.23	10.66	17.57	186.39	26.26	3.82	19.54	105.76
Electrosteel St	1831.24	−624.04	28.54	819.02	1437.47	92.33	44.73	40.08	10213.12
Total	16023.61	−672.76	2526.28	5484.23	10450.02	1346.56	589.24	585.25	30007.29

Source: Ibid.

Table 12A.2c Costs and profits of rolling mills

					Rolling mills				
	Net sales	Net profit	PBDIT	Inventory	Raw materials	Power and fuels	Employment cost	Investments	Total assets
					Rs crores				
Sujana Metals	3451.6	0.94	260.52	294.58	3104.89	46.74	21.58	147.86	2269
Sunflag Iron	1756.59	24.41	174.4	374.14	1025.3	162.79	82.06	7.67	916.9
ISMT	1504.5	−220.99	79.09	410	919.43	303.19	120.81	52.79	1472.45
Kalyani Steels	1226.82	83.31	169.81	156.06	653.42	90.07	66.41	76.82	646.84
Rathi Steels	668.82	−82.39		89.6	617.23	37.41	4.38	0.16	497.03
Surana Industries	642.18	−262.79		258.69	646.42	3.82		534.27	1927.45
TOTAL	9250.51	−457.51	683.82	1583.07	6966.69	644.02	295.24	819.57	7729.67

Source: Ibid.

Table 12A.2d Costs and profits of hot strip and cold rolling mills

	Net sales	Net profit	PBDIT	Inventory	Raw materials	Power and fuels	Employment cost	Investments	Total assets
					Rs crores				
Bhushan	10645.77	−1253.83	2177.47	7321.23	6309.84	1242.62	257.53	615.47	45761
Pennar	828.21	21.33	70.38	131.68	642.04	13.55	43.55	4.9	464.42
Steelco Gujarat	570.92	−3.13	12.56	78.99	474.5	34.81	12.78	0.05	75.92
Mahamaya	291.45	2.12	17.47	47.54	225.5	38.37	5.5	7.97	190.91
Ruchi Strips	226.76	0.06	0.24		225.99		0.29	52.95	58.88
Total	12563.11	−1233.45	2278.12	7579.44	7877.87	1329.35	319.65	681.34	46551.13
4 aggregate	12336.35								

Source: Ibid.

Table 12A.2e Costs and profits of galvanized and coated steel mills

| | | | | Galvanized and coated steels | | | | | |
| | | | | Rs crores | | | | | |
	Net sales	Net profit	PBDIT	Inventory	Raw materials	Power and fuels	Employment cost	Investments	Total assets
Uttam Galva	6952.13	30.74	541.41	1268.47	5869.47	87.74	103.06	52.87	4858.13
Jai Corp	684.49	58.36	108.51	75.95	474.77	37.4	58.16	1010.32	2006.76
Vardhaman Industries	283.34	3.5	15.37	32.85	249.77	3.21	5.2	18.76	164.07
Shree Precoated	26.12	11.93	11.98	11.17	2.15	1.83	0.63		17.64
Totals	7946.08	104.53	677.27	1388.44	6596.16	130.18	167.05	1081.95	7046.6

Source: Ibid.

Appendix III: CAPEX costs

Capital costs for integrated slab plants with continuous casting, coke, sinter plants

So far, we have only discussed the variable costs or the conversion costs of steel. Now is the time to discuss the CAPEX costs. Steelonthenet[3] has calculated some CAPEX costs as follows. For an integrated mill, capital costs describe investment for an integrated slab plant with continuous casting, typically with coke, sinter etcetera. Representative investments include:

*   CSA slab mill investment in Sepetiba, Brazil
*   CSN investment in Itaguai, Brazil
*   CVRD-Baosteel joint venture in Vitoria, Espirito Santo in Brazil
*   Sinosteel Corporation's investment in Jharkand, India

Average cost: $4300m
Average capacity: 4210 kt
Sample size: 12
Average cost/tonne: $1050/t
In terms of INR, this will be Rs 70,854 per tonne

Capital costs for iron ore integrated plants, hot strip mills and downstream rolling mills

This covers investments in ore-based integrated steel plants with hot strip production and sometimes, other additional downstream rolling capabilities. Typical examples include:

*   Wuhan Iron & Steel investment in Fangchengang Port in China
*   ArcelorMittal investment in Karnataka, India
*   Tata Steel joint venture with VSC & Vicem for investment in Vung Ang in Vietnam

Average cost: $7560m
Average capacity: 6660 thousand tonnes
Sample size: 16
Average cost/tonne: $1200/tonne, or Rs 80,916/tonne.

Notes

1   N.M. Rao. The Indian Steel Industry – Challenges and Tasks Ahead. *Iron and Steel Review.* February 2013. Kolkata.
2   Large caps include Tata Steel, SAIL and JSW. Small and medium include Jindal Stainless, Usha Martin, Mukand Steel, Kamdhenu Ispat, Adhunik Steels, Rathi Bars and Electrosteel

Ltd. Rolling mills are Suajana Metals, Sunflag Iron, ISMT, Kalyani Steels, Rathi Steels and Surana Industries. The HR/CR companies are Pennar Steel, Bhushan steel, Mahamaya Steels, SteelCo Gujarat and Ruchi Strips. The galvanized plants are Uttam Galva, Jai Corp, Shree Precoated Steels and Bardhaman Steels. These companies are the ones whose results appear on moneycontrol.com in the most complete form.

3   www.steelonthenet.com

13 The price of steel

Steel prices have a tendency to fall across the world, unable to cover the CAPEX costs, and thus, retarding both the setting up of new investments and expenditure on R&D, in order to be able to develop newer products and newer applications of steel. Since steel is also an industry with extremely high carbon emissions and has serious implications for climate issues, much of the investments in steel must compulsorily be made with regard to control of the environment. The technologies that control and manage the environment also economize heat in steel plants; retrieving, recovering and recirculating the same, around the facilities and processes. The sum and substance of the above arguments are that steel prices are far too depressed for the plants to carry on any further investments, other than those that are compulsorily made mandatory; while the slew of heat management technologies do wonders for the material and energy economy of the steel conversions, they do little else by way of expanding capacities or developing newer products for steel. In other words, steel is likely to seek greater cost efficiency and not production maximization, and this clearly tells us that steel is now a defensive industry, an industry of loss minimization and not of profit maximization, a sunset rather than a sunrise industry.

Indian prices versus global prices

The price indices across the world have decreased through the quarters of 2015 for all regions. Of these, there is relative stability in the EU and the CIS; perhaps the way they have managed their steel production and consumption through trade of both direct and indirect steel, mentioned in earlier chapters, has helped mitigate surpluses and stocks of steel. Prices appear to hold firmer in North America as well as in the EU, while China and CIS are just about afloat in terms of prices; it is India, where the price index of steel has dropped sharply. It may well be possible that Indian prices have been somewhat higher and are now being corrected.

On the whole, prices of steel across the world have fallen relative to other commodities since the 1990s, as Table 13.1 shows.

In Figure 13.1, we observe that steel prices peaked in 1980, fell and then peaked again for the last time in 1990; thereafter, steel price indices have only fallen.

Table 13.1 Price indices of carbon steel products

Price index 1997 = 100	Hot rolled coils	Cold rolled coils	Merchant bars
EU carbon steel			
15-Jan	160.2	134.6	195
15-Feb	151.3	131.9	198.1
15-Sep	143.7	127.7	194.2
15-Dec	122.2	114	180.6
Indian carbon steel			
15-Jan	117.4	125.3	106
15-Feb	103	107.4	90.3
15-Sep	96.6	105.9	89.6
15-Dec	91.8	100.1	76.6
Asian carbon steel			
15-Jan	146.2	122.7	149.6
15-Feb	123.6	103.9	134.8
15-Sep	114.5	99.1	126.6
15-Dec	103.6	92.2	117.8
North American carbon steel			
15-Jan	164.5	144.9	263.4
15-Feb	135.5	123.3	228.8
15-Sep	12.3	118.3	220.9
15-Dec	111.3	101.9	202.8
CIS carbon steel			
15-Jan	106.8	91.3	137.9
15-Feb	113.6	114.4	131.8
15-Sep	97.4	87.2	117.2
15-Dec	89.8	82.9	100.6

Source: www.meps.co.uk

Figure 13.1 The index of steel prices: global

Source: www.google.co.in/search?q=price+index+of+steel+photos&site=webhp&tbm=
isch&tbo=u&source=univ&sa=X&sqi=2&ved=0ahUKEwiz8POnjYrTAhWLuI8KHcSOC54
Q7AkIMw&biw=1093&bih=538#spf=1

Steel prices and capacity utilization rates

Steelonthenet has published a diagram on the relationship between prices and capacity utilization (Figure 13.2; clearly the lower the prices are, the lower is the utilization of capacities. Steel prices need to be above $650 in order to have over 75% of capacity utilization; at Rs 67 to a dollar, in Indian currency, this would mean Rs 43,550 per tonne of steel produced.

What do the Indian prices reflect?

The current market scenario is distorted with hefty protectionist measures, especially the Minimum Import Prices, by which the domestic prices are much higher than the import prices. Let us therefore consider the prices in 2013–14. The import and export prices are annual averages published by the JPC, while the domestic prices are of products in Mumbai for December 2013 (Table 13.2).

The domestic prices are higher for every category, except GP/GC sheets, and bars and rods and the export prices for every category are much lower than the landed costs. This simple table reveals that the Indian steel industry is uncompetitive; its prices are far above those of the imported material, a possible reason why imports are rising in the country. The exports really make no sense to the Indian steelmakers because prices in the export markets are much lower. Indian steel is, therefore, price uncompetitive. The landed cost of steel items being higher than the export prices indicate that the Indian steel market is protected. The fact that the domestic prices are higher indicates that the steel markets need even higher levels of protection. The GP/GC segment, which is the truly globalized segment of the Indian steel industry, is naturally protected against imports.

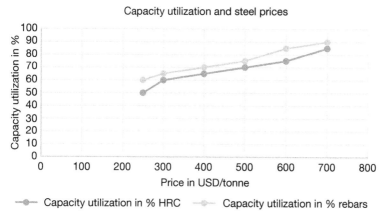

Figure 13.2 Steel prices vs. capacity utilization
Source: Metals Consulting International Limited, 2016.

Table 13.2 Landed costs, export prices and domestic prices of steel in India

2013–14	Landed costs	Export prices	Domestic price
Mild steel (prime)	*Rs/tonne*	*Rs/tonne*	*Rs/tonne*
Billets, slabs	34072	32077	41960
Re-rollable scrap	29288	35138	35450
Bars and rods	54087	42073	47610
Plates	53553	43702	49470
HR sheets	34225	41448	48010
HR coils/strp	37021	33604	48670
CR coils	45560	46325	54175
GP/GC sheets/coils	59938	52922	56050

Source: Author's calculations from JPC data.

Steel prices and raw materials: Have raw materials pushed prices of steel too high?

It is often argued that the bulk of the steelmaking costs are due to raw materials. We track the prices of raw materials over the financial year April 2015 to March 2016 against the prices of finished steel mill products to yield Tables 13.3 and 13.4.

Table 13.3 Prices of raw materials in USD per tonne

	Thermal coal	Iron ore	Electricity (in cents per kwh)	Met coke	Impact factor of thermal coal @ 1.5 tonnes	Impact for iron ore @ 1.5 tonnes	Electricity (600 units in dollars)	Met coke at 0.5 tonnes
Apr-15	61.9	51.2	6.55	94.8	92.85	76.8	393	47.4
May-15	64.7	60.2	6.65	94.8	97.05	90.3	399	47.4
Jun-15	63	62.3	6.98	94.8	94.5	93.45	418.8	47.4
Jul-15	63.4	51.5	7.3	94.8	95.1	77.25	438	47.4
Aug-15	62.8	55.4	7.32	94.8	94.2	83.1	439.2	47.4
Sep-15	58.7	56.4	7.18	94.8	88.05	84.6	430.8	47.4
Oct-15	55.9	52.7	6.87	94.8	83.85	79.05	412.2	47.4
Nov-15	56.3	46.2	6.59	94.8	84.45	69.3	395.4	47.4
Dec-15	55.9	39.6	6.42	94.8	83.85	59.4	385.2	47.4
Jan-16	53.4	41.2	6.42	93	80.1	61.8	385.2	46.5
Feb-16	54.3	46.2	6.38	93	81.45	69.3	382.8	46.5
Mar-16	55.9	55.5	6.47	93	83.85	83.25	388.2	46.5

Source: www.steelonthenet.com

Table 13.4 Prices of mill products in USD per tonne

	HRC	Plates	CRC	Wire rods	Medium structurals	Raw material factor
Apr-15	471	556	554	515	635	163.5
May-15	479	552	563	511	641	177.6
Jun-15	469	541	550	503	629	182.73
Jul-15	463	533	548	512	630	168.45
Aug-15	452	523	540	494	619	174.42
Sep-15	438	507	529	476	617	175.08
Oct-15	415	479	511	457	595	167.67
Nov-15	396	456	486	425	578	156.24
Dec-15	376	425	463	398	559	145.32
Jan-16	385	436	475	397	557	146.82
Feb-16	392	439	488	398	556	154.08
Mar-16	409	455	510	413	555	168.57

Source: Ibid.

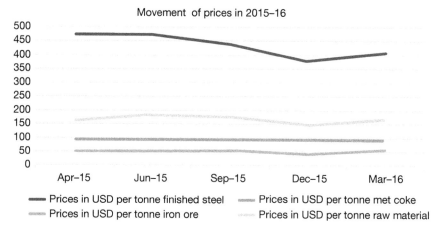

Figure 13.3 Price movement in 2015–16

In both the tables, we obtain the fact that raw material prices have really not had a telling effect on the steel margins, and despite extremely depressed market conditions, raw material prices were no more than a third of the steel prices. Margin of prices of steel were indeed good, and this perhaps explains that even given the overcapacity worldwide, steel capacity continues to be built. Steel prices can usually absorb variations in the raw material prices fairly well, at least better than the build up of excess supply of steel in the market. From the two tables and the diagram provided above, we may conclude with some confidence that markets, and not raw materials, affect steel prices. Steel prices, thus, appear to be clear of the raw material price factors.

In comparison to Table 13.3, we place the prices of steel mill products and observe that the impact of raw material costs constituted 35% of the prices of HRC in April 2015 but over 40% in March 2016. This shows that, despite the fall in prices of iron ore and coke, fall in steel prices have been sharper.

Presenting Tables 13.3 and 13.4 in the form of a graph (Figure 13.3), it becomes evident that steel prices have dipped, thus closing margins between finished products and raw materials.

Steel prices in India: historical context

Steel began to be produced in India in the 1820s, predating even the setting up of the Bessmer plants in England in 1856. If historical records are to be perused, then it appears that the modern steel industry started in colonial India (rather than in the British homeland). In the 1940s, the Government of India, still under British suzerainty, started to control the steel prices, in order to enable Indian steel companies, namely Tata Steel and Bengal Steel Corporation, later known as IISCO, to be incentivized enough to produce steel; prices were controlled, in order to ensure good margins to the steel mills, so that they could go on producing steel, add capacities and modernize facilities. The issue was to be able to ensure that the steel producers obtained "fair prices" from the British government. The "persons" who campaigned for Indian steel, were both Indian as well as British metallurgists and engineers, engaged in the business of steel production. The British government would have loved to import steel though supplies, were, indeed, affected by the war.

Immediately after the war ended, supplies of steel were once again free to move and steel prices dropped violently after 1944. During such drops, steel prices were again "fixed" by the government, in order to ensure some minimum returns so that steel mills would continue to produce steel. Since steel needs heavy investments, governments of all nations support their respective steel industries in one way or the other, and India was no exception to this trend.

Two decades later, and over a decade into Independence, the Joint Plant Committee was constituted in the year 1964, to "determine" the fair prices of steel. By this time, steel prices had skyrocketed due to war reconstruction efforts and the Second Five Year Plan was launched in India, which proposed to lay the foundation of heavy industries in the country for which steel was required. The high prices had to be managed and, here not, incentives, but now prices, were set so that the plants could cover the costs of raw materials, utilities and consumables and could also keep some mark-ups that would enable them to cover capital expenditures. Thus, the aims of setting prices for steel mills in 1944 and in 1964 were vastly different: the former was to ensure maximum prices against a regime of falling prices, while the latter was to ensure minimum prices, just enough to cover costs and a little margin for expanding capacities. The model of fixing prices in 1964 stayed on with the Indian steel companies. Interestingly, even after liberalization and the complete freeing of the steel plants, prices of steel are still determined on a cost plus basis, steel plants constantly claiming that increase in raw material prices requires the prices of mill products to increase.

Markets and prices at present

The Indian steel market is territorially divided into roughly four zones, the east, the north, the west and the south. Prices in these regions depend, primarily, upon the prices in the cities of Kolkata, Delhi, Mumbai and Chennai, respectively. In a hypothetical exercise, we may use the product mix of the steel majors and then, taking the JPC prices for a standard product in each category of production, assume the firms sell their entire output in each of the above-mentioned markets (Table 13.5). The price realizations in such hypothetical markets would have been best in the Chennai markets, and the worst in Mumbai for RINL, SAIL, Tata Steel and Essar Steel. Delhi would have been the worst for JSW, JSPL and the secondary producers. Clearly, the Delhi markets are the most crowded with steel producers and the southern markets the least.

It is interesting to note that the prices in the southern markets are higher than in the rest of India, and the prices in Mumbai are the lowest. If we reckon that the prices in the Mumbai markets are lower because of the competition from imports, then one cannot explain why Chennai markets do not face such competition.

Table 13.5 Average prices in Rs/tonne for all steel products across cities in India, December 2013

Cities	RINL	SAIL	TSL	Essar	JSWL	JSPL	Others
Kolkata	31559	32093	34158	32056	31499	29206	30931
Delhi	32172	31736	33376	31231	30698	29203	30389
Mumbai	31391	31316	31725	31223	31651	30949	31928
Chennai	32943	34134	35886	34037	33632	31290	32552

Source: Calculated from JPC data.

Table 13.6 Share of regions as percentage of total production in 2014–15

	Rerollers	HR flats	CR sheets	GP/GC/colour coated	Crude steel
East	7.88	84.00	35.45	38.60	18.92
West	64.38	14.31	38.96	53.25	15.23
North	16.75	1.69	23.60	8.16	4.56
South	10.99	0.00	1.99	0.00	61.29
Total	100.00	100.00	100.00	100.00	100.00

Source: Calculated from JPC data.

Prices have to do with availability; and steel products are more available in Mumbai than in Chennai.

Steel prices do better in regions with only large sellers, and do worse in regions with intense competition.

Steel products, like bars and rods, CR sheets and GP/GC sheets, are more available in the western segment of the country than anywhere else (Table 13.6). But, it is the south that produces the maximum crude steel, because of RINL and JSW. Incidentally, most of the traditional steel plants are located in eastern India; they produce hot rolled products, as well. The southern plants are less integrated and focus more on the production of crude steel and semis. We may infer that steel travels from the south to the west to the rerollers; HR flats travel from the east to the west to cold rollers and semis from the east also travel to the North for the rerollers. It is clear that steel travels through the length and breadth of the country, requiring rail networks, wagon capacities and roads.

The unsold stocks of steel

We have inferred, from the data analyzed in the previous chapters, that steel is in oversupply in the Indian market as well as in the world. JPC reports the unsold stocks for the year ending 2014–15 as seen in Table 13.7.

Table 13.7 Stocks at the end of March 2015

	SAIL	RINL	TSL	Essar Steel	JSWL	JSPL	Others	Total stocks
			In thousand tonnes					
Semis	21.29	1.92	35	19.77	102.82	0	183.04	363.84
Bars and rods	38.44	199.14	16	0	49.88	0	1537.74	1841.2
Plates	115.75	0	0	1.64	2.27	0	166	285.66
HR coils/strip	1430.8	0	92	44.46	196.63	0	395.22	2159.11
HR sheets	15.94	0	0	0	0	0	45	60.94
CR coils/sheets	35.36	0	0	11.47	34.27	0	452.19	533.29
GP/GC sheets	17.77	0	0	2.52	58.83	0	257.89	337.01

Source: JPC Annual Statistics 2015–16.

Table 13.8 Excess steel in the markets in 2014–15

Product category	Production for sale	Availability	Net imports	Consumption	Production less consumption	Availability less consumption
			In thousand tonnes			
Bars and rods	32251	32713	462	31081	1170	1632
Plates	4700	4873	173	4770	−70	103
HR coils/skelp	20205	20891	686	20543	−338	348
HR sheets	1138	1161	23	1113	25	48
CR coils/sheets	7509	8638	1129	8295	−786	343
GP/GC sheets	6892	5707	−1185	5554	1338	153

Source: JPC Annual Statistics 2015–16.

It is evident that stock built up is rather high for HR coils and for bars and rods, and since these are the largest product categories, in terms of quantities, it is very difficult to sustain high prices of steel, due to unsold stocks.

Table 13.8 shows the positions of excess production and excess availability of steel in the country in 2014–15. Except for GP/GC sheets, a product category which is actively exported out of India, all other categories of products are net imported. For bars and rods, there are imports despite there is already an oversupply of this product. HR coils and CR coils are underproduced, but oversupplied in the market, due to excessive imports. In fact, this observation gives credence to the contention that cheap imports of flats are retarding the setting up of indigenous capacities of HR and CR production in the country. Unfortunately, for India, since the producers do not have the right metal composition, the HR and CR produced out of such mills are not up to the standards required for automobiles and many of the consumer durables. The imports seem to be more a matter of quality than of cheaper prices.

Stocks, demand and prices

In Figures 13.4a and 13.4b, we observe that for bars and rods, import prices and stocks move more jaggedly in kinks, but for the HR coils, it is the domestic prices that move abruptly across the time intervals. This shows that, in the former,

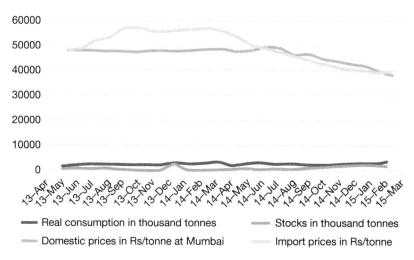

Figure 13.4a Movement of stocks and prices for bars and rods, April 2013 to March 2015

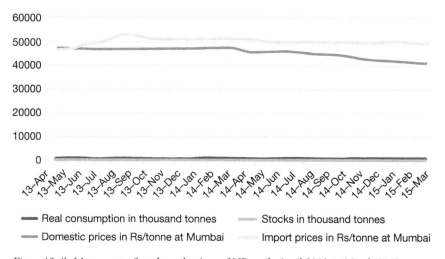

Figure 13.4b Movement of stocks and prices of HR coils, April 2013 to March 2015

import prices are used to protect the domestic prices at home, higher prices being used to constantly pull up the domestic prices. Stocks of bars and rods are adjusted, as well, to stabilize consumption. In the case of the HR coils, however, import prices have generally remained above those of the domestic prices (and the latter have strived to catch up with import prices); this has been a direct fallout of import protection (by which import prices are pegged at higher levels so that the domestic prices can catch up). Stocks are usually maintained as a steady proportion of domestic consumption.

The correlations between the ratio of stocks and consumption and imported prices and domestic prices show a fairly positive value at 0.54 for bars and rods but a negative and weak correlation at −0.40 for HR Coils. Though not conclusive enough, we may say that there are hints of imported prices increasing, with increases in the stocks of bars and rods, imports, thus, being a measure to stabilize domestic prices at home, which may fall with excess stocks. For the HR coils, the picture seems to be different, for here, the stocks have an adverse impact upon the imported prices; when imported prices drop, more stocks are brought forward in the market. This means that the HR producers hoard stocks and speculate on prices, but the producers of bars and rods use import prices to create higher price regimes for their products at home. Imposition of minimum import prices may retard the domestic production of bars and rods, as selling imported materials may become more profitable; but, for the HR producers, the minimum import prices may actually increase production at home, using the higher prices to bring forth larger supplies. This difference in behaviour may have been due to the perfect competition in the bars and rods markets, and the oligopoly in the HR segment.

Can the price of steel hold?

The fact that India needs deterrents against imports in a globalized world of free trade, shows that its prices are much higher than what prevails, ordinarily, in the world. The previous chapter clearly revealed that the costs of producing steel in India are higher than for many of the large global firms. Protection is indeed a mark of less than competitive production. It is often claimed that cheap imports (and even downright dumping by China) is the reason for prices not holding in the Indian markets. Unfortunately, this is far from the truth. The wholesale price indices published by the Government of India show that between 1994 and 2004, the steel prices were relatively higher than those of other commodities, including cereals, cotton, minerals and other metals; but, after 2004, the price of steel, relative to other commodities, started dipping, showing that the steel prices no longer had that innate urge to surge ahead; perhaps, implying a demand satiation or excess supply (Table 13.9).

The sharp rise in the price of iron and steel, relative to other commodities, made investors rush into this sector and set up facilities to manufacture iron and steel. In the period between 2005–06 and 2014–15, we witness a decline in the price of steel, with respect to other commodities, indicating that markets now tend to clear at lower prices.

Table 13.9 Price indices of various commodities

1993–94 =100	Rice	Raw cotton	Coal mining	Sugar	Cotton yarn	Cement	Iron and steel
1994–95	111	105	106	119	136	112	106
2004–05	168	223	315	163	197	153	252
2004–05 =100							
2005–06	208	90	118	109	95	102	100
2014–15	240	192	190	180	175	167	157

Source: Economic Survey, 2016, Statistical Appendices.

Conclusion

The prices of steel in India appear to be distinctly higher, when compared to global prices as well as indices of global prices. There is bound to be resistance for prices of steel to fall in India, because of the relatively lower price index of steel, compared to other commodities, like rice, sugar and cotton. Steel prices would like to rise to match similar price indices as the commodities mentioned above, and yet, due to world prices being softer, there is little scope for the Indian prices to move up. Imports of flat products have, indeed, created a downward pressure on prices, by creating adequate stocks to meet domestic demand, but imports of long products, especially bars and rods, help maintain the high prices at home, as the domestic prices are lower than those of landed costs.

Appendix I

Table 13A.1a Consumption, stocks and prices of bars and rods

	Real consumption (in thousand tonnes)	Domestic prices (in Rs/tonne) at Mumbai	Stocks (in thousand tonnes)	Import prices (in Rs/tonne)	Stocks/ consumption	Domestic price/import price
13-Apr	1685	47880	669.6	48079	0.40	1.00
13-May	2196	47760	875.9	48634	0.40	0.98
13-Jun	2296	47730	712.2	51618	0.31	0.92
13-Jul	2459	47330	912	52473	0.37	0.90
13-Aug	2352	47360	382.4	55853	0.16	0.85
13-Sep	2172	47250	350.8	55944	0.16	0.84
13-Oct	2370	47640	185.4	54453	0.08	0.87

(*continued*)

Table 13A.1a Continued

	Real consumption (in thousand tonnes)	Domestic prices (in Rs/tonne) at Mumbai	Stocks (in thousand tonnes)	Import prices (in Rs/tonne)	Stocks/consumption	Domestic price/import price
13-Nov	2266	47640	310.9	54717	0.14	0.87
13-Dec	3002	47610	2758	55082	0.92	0.86
14-Jan	2519	47820	308.3	55224	0.12	0.87
14-Feb	2668	48005	233.5	55759	0.09	0.86
14-Mar	3434	48220	209.2	54652	0.06	0.88
14-Apr	1911	47250	687.2	52616	0.36	0.90
14-May	2722	47775	891.7	49558	0.33	0.96
14-Jun	2941	49000	527.5	48467	0.18	1.01
14-Jul	2535	48650	732.9	47246	0.29	1.03
14-Aug	2763	45916	695.5	45740	0.25	1.00
14-Sep	2454	46596	1029.9	44242	0.42	1.05
14-Oct	2429	44825	1241.6	43109	0.51	1.04
14-Nov	2266	43989	1730.7	41873	0.76	1.05
14-Dec	2538	43031	1929	41069	0.76	1.05
15-Jan	2663	42433	2117.4	40730	0.80	1.04
15-Feb	2558	40357	2271.1	39851	0.89	1.01
15-Mar	3301	39027	1841.2	40120	0.56	0.97

Source: JPC and own calculations.

Table 13A.1b Consumption, stocks and prices of HR coils

	HR Coils 3.15mm					
	Real consumption (in thousand tonnes)	Domestic prices (in Rs/tonne) at Mumbai	Stocks (in thousand tonnes)	Import prices (in Rs/tonne)	Stocks/consumption	Domestic price/import price
13-Apr	1382	48455	815.2	47199	0.59	1.03
13-May	2124	48480	579	47743	0.27	1.02

			HR Coils 3.15mm			
	Real consumption (in thousand tonnes)	Domestic prices (in Rs/tonne) at Mumbai	Stocks (in thousand tonnes)	Import prices (in Rs/tonne)	Stocks/ consumption	Domestic price/import price
13-Jun	1902	48430	397.2	49952	0.21	0.97
13-Jul	1623	48385	424.8	51128	0.26	0.95
13-Aug	1896	48390	263.4	54050	0.14	0.90
13-Sep	1629	48465	254.9	53723	0.16	0.90
13-Oct	1652	48545	182.3	51934	0.11	0.93
13-Nov	1231	48655	400.4	52186	0.33	0.93
13-Dec	1786	48670	337.8	52178	0.19	0.93
14-Jan	1608	48785	421.9	52312	0.26	0.93
14-Feb	1529	48760	450.2	52463	0.29	0.93
14-Mar	1628	48760	523.2	52176	0.32	0.93
14-Apr	1647	46900	604	50877	0.37	0.92
14-May	1785	46900	533.8	49362	0.30	0.95
14-Jun	1683	47250	529.3	49610	0.31	0.95
14-Jul	1768	46813	523.7	49842	0.30	0.94
14-Aug	1699	46058	528.9	50578	0.31	0.91
14-Sep	1638	45610	682.5	50545	0.42	0.90
14-Oct	2003	44844	531.1	50185	0.27	0.89
14-Nov	1259	43444	954.5	50478	0.76	0.86
14-Dec	1733	42875	959.2	50559	0.55	0.85
15-Jan	1792	42656	1029.3	50142	0.57	0.85
15-Feb	1815	41781	921.4	49215	0.51	0.85
15-Mar	1721	41256	871.4	49547	0.51	0.83

14 Profits from steel

Excess production across the world, free trade and the regime of the WTO have ensured that, notwithstanding temporary reliefs in trade protection in the form of anti-dumping and safeguards, profits have fallen in the industry, in general. Steel, which is a matured industry, in terms of the speed of technological innovations, has stagnated and added girth in the form of excess unused capacities; profits, which are surpluses of revenues after all costs are met and dues settled, are used in capitalist systems to expand the scale of production. In times of excess capacities, profits from steel need to be not only adequate to cover costs, but also to be able to carry the idle capacities. Even if demand was to suddenly surge, profits would still be tardy, because of the technology of steel; it is so standardized that it would not take much time for capacities to be set up to wipe off demand deficits. Therefore, for profits to expand, one needs not only the swell of demand, but also a step up in technology.

The issue facing the steel industry, at present, is not really the quantum of profits, in relation to its investments or assets, but profits in relation to the other sectors of the economy. Investments are likely to flow into the steel industry from sectors with profits lower than those in steel, while investments from the steel sector are likely to go out into the sectors with higher profitability. Therefore, relative profitability of the steel industry is very important.

Relative profits of steel firms with respect to all firms

A survey of a number of firms, namely 87 selected randomly from all manufacturing sectors, and from the steel industry in the USA, EU, Japan, India, China and emerging countries, including those in the Middle East and some in South America and Africa, reveals that globally, the pre-tax profits from the 33 steel firms in India surveyed are the highest in the world, a change from our consideration of only Tata Steel and SAIL against the top steel-producing nations of the world. Among the steel firms, the USA firms trail India closely. However, when we compare the profits of all firms and those of the steel firms in each country, we find that the differences in profits are very sharp in the USA, EU, Japan, China and even the emerging markets; but, for India, the difference between the profits of all firms and the steel firms are narrower, even, the narrowest (Table 14.1).

Table 14.1 Relative pre-tax profits as percentage of net sales in steel plants and all firms in 2013

Country/region	No. of firms	Pre-tax profits all firms	No. of firms	Pre-tax profits of steel firms
USA	81	17.13	99	8.19
EU	86	8.9	96	3.11
Japan	78	4.75	89	1.41
Emerging markets	79	8.31	96	4.45
China	85	7.3	93	0.7
India	33	9.53	87	10.61
World	87	8.63	96	3.86

Source: OECD, Paris, July 2013.

Table 14.1 presents a peculiar situation; it shows that the investors in India may be indifferent between steel and other industries, as is shown when comparing the profits between steel firms and all firms. If global steel investors were to shift to India, profits for them would have expanded; no wonder then that the Japanese steel giants, the Korean giant Posco and Arcelor Mittal, the global network of firms, have been keen to invest in India, as have Alsthom and Thyssen Krupp. Were the global investors to invest in manufacturing anywhere in the world, then they would have chosen the USA. Profits across regions for all industries, except that of the USA, are more or less similar; India a bit ahead and China a bit lower. The world seems to have become truly flat, in terms of profits, and global investors may not have the incentive to travel much. But, steel posits a different picture; here, India's profits are distinctly higher than anywhere else in the world, and, in fact, provide a good scope for global investments.

Lower relative profits in the steel business

It is imperative that we now investigate into the relative profits in the steel business within India.

In Table 14.2, a brief survey of the various sectors of the economy, it is clear that the steel industry does the worst, in terms of profits among the industries mentioned; therefore, it always makes sense for promoters to move money out from steel into power, construction and even mining. The *Financial Express* of 20 March 2016 reported unrelated diversification and pulling money out of the steel business as being a major reason for loan defaults by companies, such as Bhushan Steel and others. The diversion of funds away from the steel business happened, because companies in steel wanted to graduate into sectors with higher profits.

Table 14.2 Gross margins in percentage of total revenues in India

Sector	Q4 2015	Q4 2014
Iron and steel	5.4	11.86
Metal mining	78.22	36.98
Real estate	39.78	44.59
Road transport and logistics	73.88	61.84
Marine transport	59	65.85
Electricity	47.48	57.92

Source: CSI Marketing.

Relative profits in 1994–95 and 2006–07

The two years, mentioned above, were the most remarkable years for the Indian steel industry, when capacities have grown significantly. These are also the years when there seems to have been leaps in steel innovations; in 1994–95, sponge iron and induction furnace technologies reached their respective peaks; and in 2006–07, the blast furnaces saw the most expansion, with a slew of private investors expanding capacities and setting up fresh ones in the industry. Yet, it appears from Tables 14.2 and 14.3 that steel has not been the most profitable industry in the country.

Cement and aluminum have had higher profits than steel, while steel has higher profits than cotton, food products and petroleum products. Interestingly, steel companies have diversified into cement and aluminum; JSW has set up a cement plant and Jindals have invested into Jindal Aluminum Limited. Sterlite, a Vedanta Group steel project, is actively invested in the aluminum business, as well. Ruchi Soya, Welspun Textiles and Essar Group have moved into steel, from food products, cotton and petroleum, respectively. Tata Group, which owns Tata Steel, has forays into every sector of Indian manufacturing, and in fact, Action Shoes has diversified into steel. Jupiter Steel is a diversification of a wagon company. It can be observed that investments into steel has flown in from sectors with lower profits than those of steel, while investments from steel have moved into sectors with higher profits than steel. The picture of relative profitability remains pretty much similar in 2006–07. But, the changes in the index of industrial production are important to observe.

Mining and electricity and services (which are sectors by themselves, and do not contain manufacturing) have higher profits than steel, and yet, their growth has not been commensurately high. Among the manufacturing sectors, the profits of cement have been higher than those of steel, and yet, its growth has been slower (Table 14.3). Administratively speaking, mining, electricity and even the services, have issues of permits and licenses, leases and fees, and contracts and obligations, and hence, are not as "free" as the manufacturing sectors. Perhaps, given more freedom, these sectors could grow.

Table 14.3 Profitability percentages in 1994-95: various sectors

Industry	Operating profits/gross sales	PBDIT/gross sales	PAT/gross sales	Operating profits/gross fixed assets	PBDIT/gross sales	PAT/gross sales	Operating profits/capital employed	PBDIT/capital employed
Food products	6.1	10.8	3.5	17.7	31.3	10.2	13.7	24.2
Cotton textiles	7.6	12.4	1	13.8	22.6	1.8	10.4	16.3
Petroleum products	3.3	5.8	1.9	18.7	32.6	10.9	15	26.1
Cement	10.2	15.8	3.6	12.7	19.6	4.5	16.2	19.2
Steel	7.7	14.3	3.6	8	14.8	3.7	7.5	13.9
Aluminum	19.1	30.3	13.8	13.6	21.6	9.8	14	22.3
All manufacturing	7.5	13	4	15	26.1	8.1	12.7	22.1

Source: CMIE, Corporate Sector, 1999.

Table 14.4 Profits and production growth in the various sectors

| 2006–07 | Profitability percentage | | Index of industrial production 2005–06=100 | | | | | | |
	PBDITA/total income	PAT/total income	2009–10	2010–11	2011–12	2012–13	2013–14
All manufacturing	12.5	7.6	161.3	175.7	181	183.3	181.9
Food products	11.4	5.2	133.5	142.9	164.8	169.5	167.7
Cotton textiles	16.1	1.7	127.4	135.7	134	142	148.3
Petroleum products	7.1	3.7	121.8	121.5	125.8	136.4	143.5
Cement	26.3	14.2	145.4	151.4	158.6	161.6	163.3
Steel	22.2	10.1	162.4	176.7	192.1	195.8	196.4
Mining	41.1	21.5	125	131	129	126	125
Electricity	30.9	12.3	130	138	149	155	167
Services	20.4	9.7					

Source: CMIE, Corporate Sector, 1999; Economic Survey, 2016. Statistical Appendix.

But, the industries, in terms of indices of growth, which have had the fastest growth, are food products and steel; the former, with the penultimate low profits, and the latter, with the penultimate high profits among the manufacturing sectors. Profits have been low, and technology rather rapid, to develop in food products, while profits have been somewhat high, and technology standardized, in steel, and yet, both have grown at comparable paces. This, perhaps, tells us of the rather unpredictable rules of industrial growth in which industries can grow, not really as functions of the quantum of profits, or relative profits, but, perhaps, as an outcome of the level of profits that the promoters are willing to bring forth production and capacities into the market. It may well be possible that the promoters of the food products industry, like the Chinese steel mills, are willing to be in the market at much lower profits than those of the steel industry.

Conclusion

Whether industries grow or not, may also depend on the level of profits that the promoters are willing to work for. In the case of China, promoters of the steel industry are willing to work at nearly zero margins, while those in the EU, are not willing to compromise on the levels of profits and hence, may exit the industry. The Indian scenario is a middle path between China and the EU, in which steel has expanded valiantly, despite profits in the industry being lower than that of cement. The sectors with the highest profits, namely mining, electricity and services, have stagnated, perhaps, due to the rules and laws of the country. Though the Indian steel industry has dampened much, since its peak in the 1980s, compared to the steel industry in the rest of the world, Indian steel firms earn the best profits. This may encourage the flow of foreign investments across the world into the Indian steel industry.

15 The steel trade of India

The large, integrated steel plants in India have desperately campaigned for the imposition of safeguard measures and anti-dumping duties (on supposedly cheap imports from Japan, South Korea and China) on various steel items that lead to harm to the domestic industry. It is being argued that the falling prices of steel, the underutilized capacities and the underproduced flat products are symptoms of the flood of cheap imports into India. The preceding chapters have established that overprojection of demand, and perhaps the consequential overproduction of steel, have led to the problems in the steel industry, rather than imports. The fact that import prices are lower than domestic prices across steel mill products, except for bars and rods and the galvanized flats, show that the domestic markets are not very competitive in the production of steel outside of these just mentioned products. For a brief recapitulation, we may once again refer to the data presented in Table 15.1.

Export prices are lower than the domestic prices throughout, which means that the export potential for the Indian steel sector is low, as well. Will the Indian steel industry adopt a defensive attitude of no exports and no imports?

Two questions emerge from the plight of the Indian domestic steel industry: one is whether or not imports are really cheap, and the other is whether India is competitive in exports, or not. We will first observe India's export competitiveness.

Exports and competitiveness in India's steel industry

India's trade in steel is less than a percent of the global trade in steel, as is the trade for all commodities. It is sad to imagine that a country, which had over 60% of the world trade over the Silk Road at the turn of the first millennium, is almost wiped off the map, in matters of trade. Yet, trade seems to be indispensable in a globalized world of production and investments; it is through trade that countries not only specialize and put resources to the best possible use, but also, mitigate the presently overwhelming problem of overcapacity (through production sharing, business outsourcing to areas with cheaper costs and optimization of investments through intra-industry specialization).

Table 15.1 Domestic prices, export prices and landed costs in Rs/tonne in 2013–14

Mild steel (prime)	Landed costs	Export prices	Domestic price
Billets, slabs	34072	32077	41960
Re-rollable scrap	29288	35138	35450
Bars and rods	54087	42073	47610
Plates	53553	43702	49470
HR sheets	34225	41448	48010
HR coils/strip	37021	33604	48670
CR coils	45560	46325	54175
GP/GC sheets/coils	59938	52922	56050

Source: JPC Annual Statistics 2015–16 and own calculations.

Table 15.2a India's trade in steel and other commodities in 2015–16

Region	Exports in Rs lacs		Import in Rs lacs	
	Steel	All commodities	Steel	All commodities
EU	1049872	29147644	1005514	28714319
EFTA	3839	1007433	20091	12996915
Africa	333819	16351557	326314	20617442
SACU	23205	2481895	238140	4241355
North America	321990	29574045	414907	18534406
South America	157744	4918282	220937	11558684
ASEAN	298306	16500671	588739	26030089
West Asia GCC	300012	27278450	351626	36391365
Other West Asia	232311	5179493	9102	1311783
Northeast Asia	441529	20248090	3870531	61603005
South Asia	550780	11893772	81226	1899663
CIS & Baltic	25214	1567494	281366	4634363
CARS	588	236845	7497	297995
India	3622805.36	171461770.54	7355701.36	248800747.14

Source: Export Import Data Bank of India, Ministry of Commerce.

It is clear that West Asia, South Asia, the EU and Northeast Asia are areas of heavy export of steel items (Table 15.2b). Imports are sourced from Northeast Asia, the EU, and West Asia. The EU is the favourite region for exports, while Northeast Asia is the preferred source of imports. Interestingly, the data covers ferro alloys, scrap, alloy and stainless steel all together, under chapter 72.

We may now construct another table using Table 15.2a, to obtain the share of export of steel to the export of all commodities of each region (Table 15.2c). We calculate a similar ratio for the imports, as well. In the third column, we calculate the share of trade deficit of steel in the total trade deficit. The aim of such an exercise is to be able to infer whether trade in steel helps in the cause of trade, in general, for India. The third column for trade deficit shows positive numbers (when imports are higher than exports), and hence, there is a deficit; in the case of Africa, the negative figure for trade deficit means that we have a trade surplus with the continent.

South Asia and west Asian countries, which are not part of the GCC, and the EU are regions where steel exports do very well. Northeast Asia, comprised mainly of China, Japan and Korea, does fairly well, as do South America and Africa. Yet, the

Table 15.2b Share of regions in foreign trade of India

Region	Share in total exports in %		Share in total imports in %	
2015–16	Steel	All commodities	Steel	All commodities
EU	29	17	14	12
EFTA	0	1	0	5
Africa	9	10	4	8
SACU	1	1	3	2
North America	9	17	6	7
South America	4	3	3	5
ASEAN	8	10	8	10
West Asia GCC	8	16	5	15
Other West Asia	6	3	0	1
Northeast Asia	12	12	53	25
South Asia	15	7	1	1
CIS and Baltic	1	1	4	2
CARS	0	0	0	0
India	100	100	100	100

Source: Table 15.2a.

Table 15.2c Relative advantage of India's steel exports and imports

Year 2015–16	Ratio of region's share of steel to region's share of all commodities		Share of steel in total deficit %
	Exports	*Imports*	
EU	1.70	1.18	10.24
EFTA	0.18	0.05	0.14
Africa	0.97	0.54	−0.18
SACU	0.44	1.90	12.22
North America	0.52	0.76	−0.84
South America	1.52	0.65	0.95
ASEAN	0.86	0.77	3.05
West Asia GCC	0.52	0.33	0.57
Other West Asia	2.12	0.23	5.77
North East Asia	1.03	2.13	8.29
South Asia	2.19	1.45	4.70
CIS & Baltic	0.76	2.05	8.35
CARS	0.12	0.85	11.30
India	1.00	1.00	4.83

Source: Table 15.2a.

share of steel in the overall trade deficit for EU is very high; exports, it appears, do not really help us create a favourable trade balance. There is a similar construct for imports as well. Exports to South Asia, other West Asia and the EU are important, while Northeast Asia, CIS and the Baltic and SACU countries are important for imports. Of these, the countries of "other West Asia" are the non-oil exporting countries, and SACU is comprised of the countries of southern Africa, namely South Africa, Botswana, Namibia and others. Northeast Asia consists of Japan, China and the two Koreas, whereas the CIS and Baltic countries are Russia, and the erstwhile states of the Soviet Union (in northeast Europe like Moldova, Albania, Belarus, Ukraine and others). Imports from SACU must be of high valued items, as steel has over 12% share in the total trade deficit with the region, while exports to the EU appear to be of lower value (because despite the high share of exports and modest share of imports in the region, the share of steel in the deficit is very high). Steel imports from Northeast Asia are cheaper than those from the CIS countries, as though the share of imports from the former is larger; the share of steel in the deficit is lower than what it is from the CIS countries. It is possible that we prefer to import from the Northeast countries because the steel is cheaper there.

India's free trade agreements (FTAs)

India has signed FTAs with several countries of the world; including all the countries of South Asia (Thailand, Singapore and Malaysia from ASEAN), Belarus, the Ukraine and Russia from the CIS, Bosnia Herzegovina and a broad-based trade agreement with the EU. India also has a an FTA with the EFTA countries. In South America, India has bilateral agreements with the Mercusor countries and separately, with Chile. In Northeast Asia, it has comprehensive economic partnership agreements with South Korea and Japan, and negotiations are under way for Mongolia. The impact of such free trade is yet to be studied, and the benefits yet to be established. But, recalling our data from previous chapters, export prices of steel items are the lowest, while the landed costs of imports are lower than the domestic prices; hence, the exposure of the Indian steel industry to the global commodity flows has not been very beneficial. Sections of the Indian steel industry have appealed to the Ministry of Steel to take steel out of the FTAs.

If we observe the imports into the SACU, Northeast Asia and CIS and the Baltic countries from which India's imports of steel products seem to be relatively significant, steel seems to contribute heavily. SACU countries, namely South Africa, Lesotho, Botswana and Namibia and the CIS and the Baltic countries, are huge sources of scrap and hot rolled coils, respectively. India is negotiating free trade agreements with SACU, as a whole, and the individual countries of the CIS.

A brief survey of FTAs with Malaysia, Singapore, Thailand, Japan and South Korea reveal that, in no case, is steel included in the tariff list marked out for concessions; steel appears to be pretty much outside of the FTAs.[1]

Briefly surveying imports from the countries with whom FTAs are the most active, namely Malaysia, Japan, South Korea and Thailand, as well as from China, for three consecutive years, we observe that in comparison to the average import prices from all countries, none of the countries mentioned above have consistently sold steel cheap, except China. It was only in 2013–14 that Japan sold cheap to India, but never after that (Table 15.3).

Table 15.3 Import of carbon and alloy steel (excluding defectives and seconds)

	2015–16		
	Value in Rs crores	*Quantity in thousand tonnes*	*Unit value in Rs/tonne*
Japan	8664.21	2195.41	39465.11
South Korea	10325	3083.98	33479.46
Malaysia	543.65	80.44	67584.54
Thailand	173.44	41.85	41443.25
All Countries	47192.85	12691.93	37183.35
China	13937.44	4131.46	33734.90

	Value in Rs crores	Quantity in thousand tonnes	Unit value in Rs/tonne
		2015–16	
		2014–15	
Japan	8056	1601.93	50289.34
South Korea	9085.05	1926.65	47154.65
Malaysia	535.41	105.3	50846.15
Thailand	116.64	15.93	73220.34
All Countries	47000.13	10016.59	46922.29
China	15263.32	3610.47	42275.16
		2013–14	
Japan	6648.59	1358.09	48955.44
South Korea	6948.97	1320.83	52610.63
Malaysia	241.48	32.83	73554.68
Thailand	141.27	21.89	64536.32
All Countries	31208.03	5708.18	54672.47
China	5562.97	1088.44	51109.57

Source: JPC Annual Statistics 2015–16.

Normalized revealed comparative advantage of steel

The Exim Bank has calculated the normalized revealed comparative advantage of iron and steel exports to various regions across the world (and presented in Figure 15.1) is the diagrammatic representation of the findings. It is observed that a larger percentage of commodities, under the category of iron and steel, have suffered from decreased advantage (than the proportion of commodities which have shown increases in revealed comparative advantage). The exports that are destined for Oceania have done better than anywhere in the world, while those destined for Latin America have shown no change. We may conclude that steel exports from India are not very competitive, and an increase in exports may finally lead to loss of resources, while the exact opposite, which is the import of steel, may be beneficial to the economy at large.

Conclusion

The fact that India is less competitive in the export of steel may mean that India is less competitive in the manufacture of steel. An expansion in capacities to manufacture steel may lead to losses for the economy, as a whole. The loss of competitiveness

Net revealed comparative advantage for steel exports
from India to the world 2008–2015

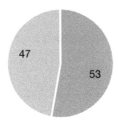

▨ Percentage of steel products in which there is a decrease in NCRA

▨ Percentage of steel products in which there is an increase in NCRA

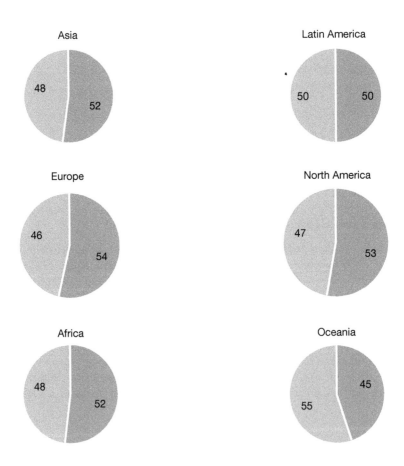

Figure 15.1 Net revealed comparative advantage of exports of steel products
from India 2008–2015

Source: Exim Bank, 2016.

in steel may be related directly to the state of depressed demand for steel, and therefore, lower margins, and hence, lower incentives for investments into technology and development. The slowing down of demand may well be said to be the sole reason for the loss of competitiveness in steel.

In times of increasing demand for steel, margins expand, prices of steel relative to other commodities rise, returns on investments rise progressively and competitiveness increases through investments in technology. If demand falls, prices of steel fall relative to other commodities, profits shrink, margins contract and technological innovations stall for which competitiveness falls. During this phase, the exports lose out on their revealed comparative advantage.

Note

1   Lok Sabha Question Number 9671, November 2016.

Conclusion
Summary of arguments

We are now in a position to recapitulate and conclude the arguments we made around the policy objective of the Indian steel industry, which is to incessantly increase the capacity and production of steel (from the present 100 million tonnes) to some 300 million tonnes, not so far in the future. Production targets have been revised downwards, to accommodate realities of the Indian economy to its fantasies of an endless growth, but, on the whole, to increase production, monotonically, has been the principal aim of the Indian steel policy. The monograph has been a critique of such an aim. The chapters in this book have argued that it is better to aim for the maximization of value for the steel industry (rather than increase steelmaking capacities). The problem of expanding steelmaking capacities lie, partly, in the excess capacities, which have developed in the world, and partly, in the fact that the Indian steel industry does not seem to be too competitive (which means expansion of production will be self-defeating).

The other obsession of the Indian policy makers in the steel industry is the belief that it is only the integrated steel mills that are technologically competent and must be encouraged. The integrated mills utilize their capacities better, have lower costs and make more profits (and indeed, during the days of laying the foundation of the Indian steel industry, which was before even Independence, it was the integrated mill that was looked upon as the core of modern technology); the numerous smaller players were considered to be necessary evils, filling in the spaces created by demand gaps, soon to be eliminated, when the integrated plants grew in capacities. A possible reason for encouraging the growth of the integrated steel mills has also, been a desire on the part of the policy makers to eliminate the smaller players. Tracking technology growth in India, we observe that if there has been a genuine growth of indigenous technology, then it has been around the electric furnaces and sponge iron producers of the country; in other words, the smaller players have led the technology growth in the country. The large integrated plants have merely adopted technologies, most of which, they have imported from abroad. The growth of the small sector of steel production, from a mere 15% of the steel production in 1980s, to presently over 50%, is the result of the high technology growth among the smaller producers; indeed, it is on the shoulders of the smaller producers that India emerged from the tenth largest steelmaking nation, in 1991, to the third, in 2016.

If the large integrated steel producers have grown, they have grown without the commensurate technology advances; and hence, expanded debts and overheads, without bringing in the innovations to reduce variable costs. The favour of the policy makers towards the large integrated sector may, therefore, mean a swelling of company debts, overcapacity and loss of competitiveness, precisely, due to the absence of backup of technological innovations.

Tracking the excess capacity in India in terms of steel mill products, we find that the hot rolled coils, which are produced by the large integrated plants, as well as the large mills in the electric arc furnace sector, are undersupplied. Since these are also costlier in India, as compared to the imported material, it is unlikely that more hot rolled coils will be produced in India, until and unless, stiff levels of protective barriers (in the form of anti-dumping duties and safeguard duties) are imposed. But, the artificial raising of prices may harm the downstream producers, who use the hot rolled coils as their inputs. Further, we may construe the higher domestic prices of hot rolled coils as a sign of being globally uncompetitive. If we are to encourage the production of hot rolled coils in the country, we may encourage a rather uncompetitive line of production. The monograph recommends imports, because, were the cold rolled coil and galvanized coil producers to use imported hot rolled coils, then, the margins would really improve. It might be a better idea for the Indian steel industry to improve the value of the industry than to merely add tonnage (by way of increased production and capacity).

If, the ratio of landed costs to the domestic price is an indication of innate competitiveness in the Indian markets, then a ratio lower than one means the products (for which the landed costs are lower than those of the domestic prices) are inherently uncompetitive. Bars and rods and galvanized flat steel are competitive in India, and so are the plates; but, for the rest of the products, India would do better to import. Incidentally, bars and rods and galvanized steel are produced, overwhelmingly, by the smaller producers in the electric arc furnace, while plates are produced by the integrated mills using the oxygen route for steelmaking. Choice of product mix also entails a choice of technology. Were India to produce some steel and import some as all, then one would have to export those products, which one makes at home, in order to have the money to buy those which are not produced domestically. Unfortunately, Indian export price realizations, across the board, are far lower than the domestic prices, and hence, exports may actually mean the overall lowering of economic benefits. A way out of this impasse is to specialize among the various segments of the steel industry within the country, namely the integrated mills would produce more plates and slabs, while the smaller producers could produce more bars and rods and galvanized sheets, the last of which would be processed out of imported hot rolled coils and so on.

Specialization between the large and the small plants was, in fact, in the original scheme of things, in the days of the industrial licenses and price controls. The integrated plants would manufacture semis, while the smaller plants would roll them out; things slowly changed, despite the controls, when, in the 1980s, demand increased (and more steel needed to be produced). Scrap import was allowed, and electric arc furnaces, once more, emerged in India and have been growing ever since. These smaller furnaces were meant to fill in the gaps in the supply of steel for the downstream processors; something that the integrated steel mills were meant to do, but did not, for they started processing value added products themselves. The large and small plants entered into a competition with one another instead of cooperation. The rolling mills were starving because the integrated mills, instead of supplying semis to them, were now producing the thinner and lighter mill products. The smaller plants were now left to the task of making steel semis to fill in the gaps left by the integrated mills. The capacity of steelmaking in the country rose because of the transformation of relations from cooperation into competition. Since the 1980s, competition has been rising, and so is steelmaking capacity; it has gone beyond, perhaps, what the country needs or can afford, pushing us into a state of overcapacity.

Policy makers argue that, as India develops more and more, it will need more and more steel, and one must, then, plan for that magical 300 million tonnes. Though India is the third largest steelmaking country in the world, it has one of the lowest per capita steel consumptions, and were it to grow to the 180 kgs of average consumption, India would need three times as much as steel; hence, an increase from the present 100 million tonnes to 300 million tonnes. There is little merit in this argument, really, because the production of steel is not always related to a country's economic development; instead, it is determined by a myriad of factors pertaining to technological capabilities, organizational abilities and the willingness to produce steel (as an activity in which resources are employed better than what they would have been in competing industries). Relative profits of steel are an important determinant in whether a country decides to produce its own steel. The per capita steel is a division of the total steel produced by the population; and, one of the features of countries that have higher per capita steel use is perhaps, a lower population.

Indian iron ore is rich in ferrous content, but is also high in phosphorous. This makes it very useful for the production of flat steel, but not for long products; this is where, perhaps, the logic of promoting flat steels becomes important. Flat steels, because of the dimensions, can best be produced in large plants, and large plants would do better were they to be in the oxygen route; hence, the policy makers favour the large integrated steel mills, which could manufacture hot rolled products. But, not only are the hot rolled wide sheets underproduced, they are more expensive to produce in India, which thus, accounts for lower capacity utilizations. The monograph finds a reason for this paradox, which is technology. The slew of indigenous technological innovations, which lie at the heart of competitiveness of the steel industry, have been championed by the small sector; the large sector has mainly imported technology and adapted these in terms of plant and machinery (and not processes into their plants). This is why, while the growth of the small sector is organic, the growth of the large sector has been extraneous.

The mounting bad loans of the steel industry, which eventually led to the present day demonetization (and a cash crisis in the economy as banks have been turned empty through loans that were never paid back), makes us take a hard look at current steel policy. We should consider, especially in the face of excess capacities across the world and cheap steel from China, whether we should hold on to a century-old thesis that steel production should follow demand for steel in the country, or whether we should focus more on steel backed by excellent technology innovations at home, and not by state of the art technology, imported from abroad.

Index

For Product Safety Concerns and Information please contact our EU
representative GPSR@taylorandfrancis.com
Taylor & Francis Verlag GmbH, Kaufingerstraße 24, 80331 München, Germany